COTSWOLD HERITAGE

Aston Subedge, where the plains meet the hills

COTSWOLD HERITAGE

by LOUISE WRIGHT

with drawings by JAMES PRIDDEY

ROBERT HALE LIMITED   LONDON

© *Louise Wright and James Priddey 1977*
First published in Great Britain 1977

Reprinted 1979

ISBN 0 7091 6223 5

Robert Hale Limited
Clerkenwell House
Clerkenwell Green
London EC1R 0HT

PHOTOSET AND PRINTED
IN GREAT BRITAIN BY
REDWOOD BURN LIMITED
TROWBRIDGE AND ESHER

Contents

COMPANION VOLUMES

Heart of England by Louise Wright and James Priddey
Rural Kent by John Boyle and John Berbier
Sussex Scenes by Michael H. C. Baker
Somerset Scenes by Aylwin Sampson

Illustrations

ILLUSTRATIONS

Acknowledgements

For permission to quote from the works named, I would like to thank:

Richard Courtauld (the new edition of "I Chanced to Rove"); Roger Lancelyn Green (Gordon Bottomley's "King Lear's Wife"); Laurie Lee (books and poems); Patrick Harvey (the poems of F. W. Harvey); D. Badham-Thornhill (the poems published in "People Within"); Sir George Trevelyan (his address on the Sapperton Group); Williamson Music Ltd (excerpts from "Oh What a Beautiful Mornin' ").

For their kind help:

The Cotswold District Council; at the Gloucestershire County Council, the Archivist, the County Surveyor and the Planning Officer; the Librarians at the Birmingham Reference Library, the Birmingham Midland Institute and the Gloucester County Library; the staff at Beshara, Swyre Farm; Light for the World, at Northwick Park; the Society for Industrial Archaeology; Bryant Feddon Workshops and Winchcombe Pottery.

My special thanks to my many friends in the Cotswolds who gave their time so generously:

Colonel and Mrs Claud Biddulph, Mr and Mrs F. Russell Cox, Mr and Mrs Lees-Milne, Mr and Mrs Charles Taylor, Mr and Mrs David Verey. Mrs D. H. Binney, Mrs Helen Butlin, Miss Alice Coates, Miss Angela Gibson, Mrs Guy Griffiths, Miss Rosamund Hogg, Miss Nancy Jewson, Mrs Jean Keyte, Miss Doris Lindner, Miss Nora Marshall, the Prioress of Burford Abbey, Mrs Jeanne Renshaw, Miss Nora Yoxall.

R. E. Adlard, L. E. Arkell, Frank Baldwin, Norman Bucknall, A. Collett, Sir Anthony Denny, Crispin Gill, Henry Hart, Joe Henson, Michael Hope, Phillip Lee, Theo Merrett, Jack Nelson, Paul Nicholas, R. J. Nicholas, A. D. Nichols, Edward Payne, Frank Reitz, Sir Gordon Russell, Owen Scrubey, Sir George Trevelyan, Simon Verity, Andrew Wood.   L. W.

To
Old Herbaceous
　　　　(L. W.)
and

To
the Members and Associates
of the Royal Birmingham
Society of Artists on the
occasion of the 150th
anniversary of the
founding of their society
　　　　(J. P.)

Introduction

Cotswold country is unique. It makes an immediate impression, for its heights are bold, its upland views wide and its valleys steep and well wooded. To discover the real charm of the Cotswolds, one must explore the byways as well as the highways, sit awhile in the old churches, enjoy the company in the small village pubs and talk with its people. But warily! One eager townee extolled the beauty of the countryside, the freshness of the breezes, saying heartily—"Not many deaths around here I'll be bound." "No," came the laconic reply. "We only die once in these parts."

I have ranged over the Cotswolds since my student days, wandering from one village to the next at all seasons of the year, sketching and bird-watching and, as the Cotswold poet W. H. Davies advised, finding it rewarding "to stand beneath the boughs, and stare as long as sheep or cows".

The beauty of the Cotswold buildings stems from the geological structure of the land. The limestone hills were formed millions of years ago, when the enormous pressure of earth movements pushed up the sea bed, eventually resulting in a great escarpment. This ridge of solid limestone, known as oolite, or eggstone, because of its formation of rounded grains which resemble hard roe, rises steeply to 800 feet in the escarpment above the Vale of Evesham; whereas on the south-eastern side the hills take nearly twenty miles to slope away to the Oxford plain. Throughout the area, it is the limestone, ranging in colour from pale yellow to a rich tan brown and greying with age, which dominates the scene, giving the Cotswold country endearing and enduring harmony. In medieval times, most of the villages had a quarry and near the larger villages there were, and still are, extensive beds of good stone. It is the type and quality of the stone which governs its use as a building material. The shelly types break in an irregular way and are used mainly for drystone walling. Building stone is obtained from deeper beds. It is easily cut and dressed, hardens with age and exposure and, when skilfully laid with the grain, it rarely crumbles. Some of the beds are composed of thin layers. These can be split by the action of frost, to make tilestones. Expertly graded by the slatters, they were ranged on the roofs, from the 'Long Sixteens' (24 inches long),

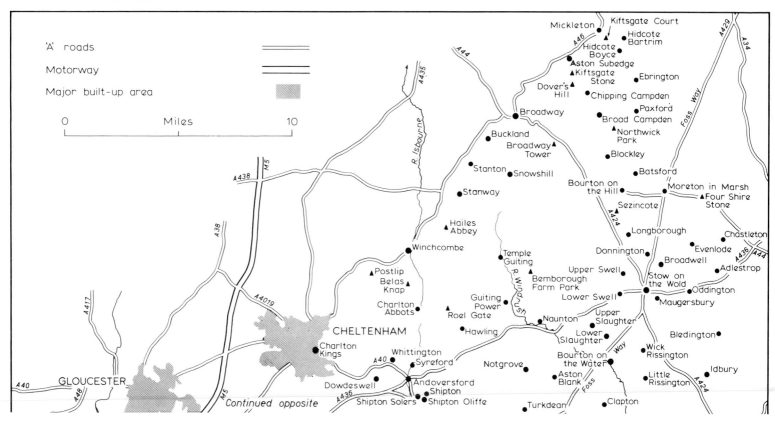

'A' roads

Motorway

Major built-up area

0   Miles   10

Mickleton

Kiftsgate Court

Hidcote
Bartrim

Hidcote
Boyce

Aston Subedge

Kiftsgate
Stone

Ebrington

Dover's
Hill

Chipping Campden

Broadway

Paxford

Broad Campden

Buckland

Northwick
Park

Broadway
Tower

Blockley

Stanton

Snowshill

Batsford

Stanway

Bourton on
the Hill

Moreton in Marsh

Four Shire
Stone

Sezincote

Hailes
Abbey

Longborough

Chastleton

Winchcombe

Temple
Guiting

Donnington

Evenlode

Broadwell

Adlestrop

Postlip
Belas
Knap

Upper Swell

Bemborough
Farm Park

Stow on
the Wold

Charlton
Abbots

Guiting
Power

Lower Swell

Oddington

Roel Gate

Naunton

Maugersbury

Upper
Slaughter

Hawling

CHELTENHAM

Lower
Slaughter

Bledington

Charlton
Kings

Whittington

Wick
Rissington

Notgrove

Bourton on
the Water

GLOUCESTER

Syreford

Aston
Blank

Little
Rissington

Idbury

Dowdeswell

Andoversford
Shipton

Shipton Solers

Shipton Oliffe

Turkdean

Clapton

Continued opposite

R. Isbourne

R. Windrush

Foss Way

A 429

A 34

A 44

A 435

M5

A 438

A 38

A 417

A 4019

A 436

A 424

A 40

A 48

M5

A 436

A 46

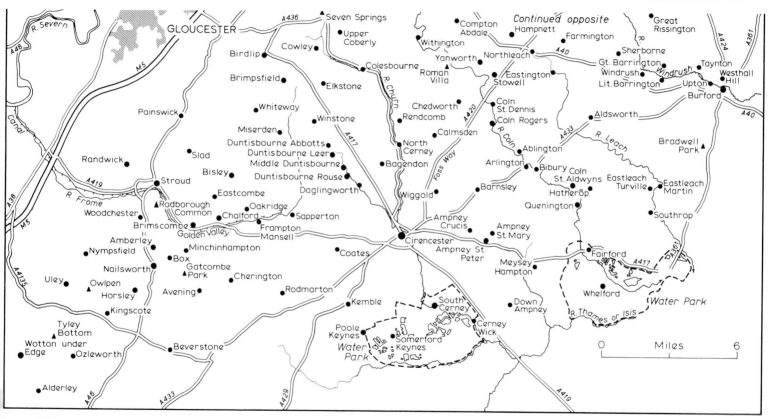

overhanging the walls in lieu of gutters, up to the smallest tiles called 'Cussoms', awkward to fit under the ridge stones.

Seen from surrounding hills, the roofs of Cotswold villages complement the walls of the buildings. The beauty of a Cotswold village owes as much to the integral use of its native stone as to the siting of the village or to the skill of its stonemasons. Their skills have been handed down unchanged through centuries of change, beginning with those masterly stonemasons, the Romans, whose towns and villas graced the Cotswolds. Remains of the Roman city of Corinium, called 'The Crossroads of Britain', are visible in Cirencester, and their famous Fosse Way, linking Aqua Sulis (Bath) with Lindum (Lincoln), continues in use as one of the main roads across the Cotswolds. After the Romans and the Saxon invaders, there came those other master-builders, the Normans, whose work and influence is to be seen in many of the churches. After the Norman Conquest, William I rewarded with gifts of land those friends and relations who had fought with him. He also endowed some French religious foundations with English land. Thus many Cotswold manors came into the possession of French monasteries. By the reign of Henry V, at which period so much of France belonged to England, William's endowments were transferred, to enrich the established English abbeys.

It was the great religious communities which improved the strain of the sturdy sheep by crossing them with the heavily fleeced Flemish rams. For 300 years, Cotswold fleeces were England's greatest export until the fourteenth century, when the villagers began to acquire their cloth-weaving skills. The religious establishments improved agricultural methods and provided varied employment for many of the villagers; the thousands of pilgrims who journeyed to the holy shrines, particularly at Hailes Abbey, may be regarded as the pioneers of the Cotswold Tourist trade.

After the Dissolution of the Monasteries, much land and well-dressed stone became available for grander manor houses and larger farms. The unemployed master masons from the abbeys travelled from village to village, offering their highly prized services, particularly to those wool staplers and clothiers who, like the monasteries, had grown rich from trading the heavy fleeces. These wealthy men ordered fine stone houses for themselves and good cottages for their workers. They enlarged and enhanced the churches to the greater glory of God, not forgetting to perpetuate their own names on tombs of singular magnificence, but bequeathing a wide heritage of beauty which remains remarkably unspoilt.

For, despite all the changes, and the increasing tempo of life, as packhorse gave way to coaches, canals and railways, and these to motor vehicles, the Cotswolds persist as a largely agricultural area. If road traffic and tourism can be controlled, then the Cotswolds may be safe for the future. The Department of the Environment, the Countryside Commission, the National Trust, and many small local societies all work together to preserve this heritage. BUT, it is also the responsibility of all who enjoy the district, to support this work and leave no litter.

The region has no fixed boundaries, each admirer must make his own. Mine spreads from the wolds above the Vale of Evesham across to Burford and southwards to where the wooded valleys of The Bottoms slope towards Wotton-under-Edge and Alderley. I have described my ellipsoidal zigzag tour for the benefit of the motorist using a car merely to get from place to place. The best way to enjoy any country is on foot or on horseback. The Cots-

wolds are rich in well-signposted foot and bridle paths, including the 100 miles of The Cotswold Way. Thanks to the Gloucestershire County Council and the Ramblers' Association, this walk is well signposted from Chipping Campden, along the escarpment to the Stroud valleys and The Bottoms. It leaves my Cotswold country at Alderley and continues to Bath.

Ordnance Survey maps are essential for anyone who wishes to know the countryside. My well-worn 1 inch series has been replaced by the 1974 metric 1:50,000 scale, or for walkers, the 1:25,000, on which field boundaries, villages, isolated buildings, lanes, footpaths and contours are all clearly shown. The maps on pages 14 and 15 show the overall area covered by this book. They are based on the Ordnance Survey. Walkers are advised to use *The Cotswold Way, a Walker's Guide* by Mark Richards.

*Chipping Campden High Street. The Market Hall, presented to the town by
Sir Baptist Hicks, Viscount Campden, in the seventeenth century*

CHAPTER ONE

Up to the Wolds

'Unscabbarded against the sky
The blue high blade of Cotswold lie.'

Approaching from the north, the first signs of Cotswold stone are in the vale villages of Mickleton and Aston Subedge. The manor house at Aston Subedge was the home of Endymion Porter, a patron of the early Stuart poets and of Robert Dover.

At Weston Subedge, the steep road to the hills leaves the low road and in minutes, the vales are 700 feet below and there are the walks on Dover's Hill. The wind blows, the turf is springy; from the topograph, one can trace the sweep of the vales from Warwick Castle to Radnor Forest. One walk follows the ridge of land which forms a semi-circle round the great natural arena whereRobert Dover held his 'Olimpick Games'. A stone relief on the memorial in the car park depicts Robert Dover as he rode on a white

The Manor House at Aston Subedge, home of Endymion Porter, born 1575. Prince Rupert is said to have stayed here for Robert Dover's Games.

horse, wearing his borrowed finery, to open the games. The bronze plate beneath the relief explains: "Robert Dover, 1575–1641. On this hill top, Robert Dover's Olimpick Games were celebrated from about 1612–1852, when they were stopped by the enclosure of Weston Subedge".

A stone relief on the memorial on Dover's Hill shows Robert Dover riding out to open his 'Olympick Games'

The jovial, exuberant, public-spirited Dover was an attorney, who after his marriage lived at Barton, near Moreton-in-Marsh. He was a man "Nimble in exercise and most at home in the saddle". With the help of his many famous friends and particularly of Endymion Porter of Aston Subedge, Groom of the Bedchamber to James I, Dover obtained the King's permission to hold the games.

At the opening ceremony, Dover rode out of his portable wooden castle, attired in the King's cast-off finery, to a salvo of two cannon, fired from the wooden castle's twin towers—and the games began. Thursday of Whitsun week was chosen for the opening day, a revival of the old custom, the Cotswold Whitsun Ales. The games lasted three days and the event was intended not only for local merry-making, but also, in its heyday, as a gathering of distinction, attracting great sportsmen to compete for valuable prizes on the 500 acres of unenclosed land.

The favourite local sport was the simple shin-kicking contest, village team against village team. Ben Jonson wrote:

> The Cotswold with the Olympic vies
> In manly games and goodly exercise.

The finale of the games was the Scuttle-brook Wake, held in the streets of Chipping Campden on the Saturday of

Whitsun week. This still survives, with its stalls and modern merry-go-rounds.

Whitsun was also a survival of the old pagan spring festival of sun worship, the time when the sun brought new life to the earth. The people, who greeted the spring with joy, danced, decorated their horses and crowned any ricks which had survived the winter. They ate, drank and made merry, until Puritanism put a stop to all this unseemly frivolity.

With the building of some railways in the Cotswolds, gangs of navvies were brought in and lodged in the surrounding villages. During the five years spent on the construction of the Mickleton tunnel, the lawlessness of the navvies was a great problem and the games were the high-spot of their bored existence. Hundreds of their friends came from Birmingham and the Black Country for the horse racing and to join in the fun, and alas, the games ceased to be fun. The great crowds, the unsporting brawls and drunken vandalism, were too much for the quiet countryside. They shocked the Victorian conscience, and largely due to the influence of Canon Bourne, Rector of Weston Subedge, the games were stopped and the land enclosed.

Now, thanks to the efforts of two men who devoted much of their time and money to the preservation of the Cotswolds, the land has been acquired by the National Trust. Today, picnickers play their family games on Dover's Hill and walkers take the path along the ridge, over the stile to Kingcomb Lane, down the Hoo (a Saxon word meaning the heugh or spur of a hill) into Chipping Campden.

This is one of the many elegant towns in the Cotswolds. The mile-long curving High Street is graced on either side by the houses of its wealthier inhabitants, dating from the fourteenth century onwards and built of local stone. This golden stone, which mellows to a warm grey, has been quarried for centuries and each village at some time had a local quarry. The Campden quarries on Westington Hill have been worked since the Middle Ages. The old quarry is now overgrown with trees and flowers, the haunt of jays, badgers and lizards. A few outcrops of the oolitic limestone, streaks of yellow and white still uncovered by the rampage of nature, show high up in the bushes.

The new part of the quarry, which I was kindly allowed to visit, was busy with men operating all kinds of gigantic yellow machines, which grabbed viciously at the golden stone. Lorries, which have replaced the old hand-pushed trucks on rails, waited to take the stone to the contractors. The lorrymen sat in their cabs, the inevitable transistor blaring beside them, momentarily drowned by the blasts from the gelignite.

During the last forty years, the cutting of the new

21

quarry has advanced into the hillside in the direction of Campden. As the deep strata are exposed, they show clearly the deposits of millions of years when this area was part of the sea bed. In the sunlight, with heavy cast shadows, the variety of colour and the horizontal formations of the newly exposed face behind a fall of blasted stone, make a rare subject for a painting. At the entrance to the new quarry are the relics of the old mine quarryings which form great warrens under the hill. They have been closed for many years; the last stone taken from them was used for the Campden War Memorial.

In the Middle Ages, great flocks of sheep grazed over this fine underlying building stone and it was the wool from these which enriched the merchants and enabled them to pay for their large and elegant stone houses. The wool was carried out of Campden by way of the turnpike alongside the Noel Arms, through the southern counties to the ports.

On first seeing the High Street of Chipping Campden, you are spoiled for choice. Take a walk along this wide street, up one side and down the other, looking at the opposite side, in order best to appreciate the craftsmanship of the stonemasons and their innate appreciation of the materials with which they worked. Look up at the variety in the stonework, at the sundials, at the roofs—steeply pitched because the local tile-stones are slightly porous.

Chipping Campden, over the centuries, owes much of its present beauty to the men who have chosen to live there. One of the earliest was William Grevel, who in 1390 built Grevel House, with its gargoyles, sundial and slender bay windows. He was a wealthy wool stapler, whose family had lived in Campden for many years and whose descendants became the earls of Warwick.

Across from Grevel House is the Wool Staplers' Hall, built a few years before Grevel House by the wool-trading Calf family. Merchants gathered here from far and near to buy the staples of Cotswold wool. The Hall may be visited during the summer months and it houses an extraordinary collection of museum objects. Apart from all the interesting items of local domestic life, including pictures and photographs relating to Campden and its people, there are scientific instruments, a Jaguar engine, relics of the early cinemas, typewriters, phonographs, cameras and the beautiful bottles and jars once used by apothecaries.

The wool merchants met in the large hall on the first floor, with its magnificent roof and stone fireplace, over which is one of the few crude items of craftwork to be found in Campden—the arms of the Calf family.

The small stained-glass window high in the eaves is much later than the original house and is part of the restoration undertaken by C. R. Ashbee, who lived at the

The almshouses on Church Street, Chipping Campden. The street leads to the parish church of St James and to one of the remaining gatehouses of the home of Sir Baptist Hicks

Hall when he moved with his Guild of Handicrafts from London to Campden in 1902. The motif he chose for the stained-glass window was his favourite Ash and Bee.

On exhibition in the great hall is one of the earliest balloons and a parachute made by Marie Merton. She joined the white calico with bands of red, using a fine herring-bone stitch and embroidering her name on the bottom band. She was one of a group of girl parachutists trained to jump from balloons at a height of 10,000 feet by Lieut. Lempriere in the 1880s. They climbed out of the rickety basket below the balloon and jumped, clutching desperately to the hoop of their 'chutes', quite as brave and spectacular in their time as our modern troop of lady skydivers.

In revolting contrast are those diabolical inventions, mantraps, used extensively against poachers until made illegal by an Act of Parliament in 1827.

The original Wool Staplers' Hall consisted of two rooms, the upper and more important hall being approached by an outside staircase, long since demolished; the doorway is now a window. The bow window facing the street is thought to be a later addition. The other museum rooms are part of Bedfont House, added and converted over the years by members of the Griffith family, who have lived there for centuries—in the case of Mr Scudsmore Griffith, for one century and two weeks. The

family opened the premises as a museum which they filled with a vast collection of their treasures, adding to them year by year.

In the past, whenever Campden's fortunes have been at a low ebb, benefactors have appeared to restore them. Following the Calf family and the Grevels came Sir Baptist Hicks, a founder of the East India Company, one of the richest men in the country and a friend of the new king, James I. He bought the Manor of Campden from Anthony Smythe, whose father's tomb may be seen in the church. Sir Baptist not only built a magnificent if rather flamboyant house for himself, but also gave money for the benefit of the people of Campden. Outside the gates of his own house, he built and endowed the almshouses, a row of buildings providing accommodation for twelve persons. This row, with eight bays and four centre-arched doorways, is considered a fine example of the Cotswold mason-craft of the early seventeenth century. The almsmen and women formerly wore a traditional coat with Sir Baptist's crest of a buck's head, embroidered in silver on the sleeve. In 1612, he built a small Jacobean conduit (still to be seen on Westington Hill, opposite the quarry) to provide a water supply for the inmates of the almshouses. He also gave to the town the now famous Market Hall, often called the Wool Market, although it was used as a general market for the sale of local produce. The word

'Chipping' derives from the Saxon *ceapon*, meaning to barter.

Charles II, on his escape from Boscobel to Bristol disguised as Jane Lane's servant, is reputed to have drunk too freely of Campden ale and to have quarrelled with a farmer in the Market Hall, only being saved from appearing before the justices by making profuse apologies, urged on him by the ever-watchful Jane.

It was Sir Baptist who gave new life to the grammar school and provided the fine Flemish lectern and carved Jacobean pulpit in the church. Instead of the more usual lectern eagle, a falcon with an open beak supports the Bible, to the fascination of school-children and many a passing visitor. There seems to be a great temptation to feed him coins and sweetwrappers.

Sir Baptist was regarded as an upstart by the older Gloucester gentry, but by lending money to the Crown he won favour at court. In 1626, he was made Baron Hicks of Ilmington and Viscount Campden. He had no sons and his titles passed to his daughter Juliana's husband, Edward, Lord Noel. The Noel Arms, opposite the Town Hall, was probably a private house in the fourteenth century, before first becoming the George Inn and later Campden's oldest hotel, The Noel Arms. In the large courtyard at the rear is the stone staircase which in coaching days led to the coachmen's quarters above the stables.

Bedfont House, an eighteenth-century building next to the Wool Staplers' Hall, is of a later period than Campden's other distinguished houses. It was built in the 1740s for the Cottrell family by Thomas Woodward, at that time the lessee of the Campden quarry. An old story tells how he looted the stone ornaments for the house from the ruins of Norton Hall, after the fire there in 1741.

Until about 1831, Cattlebrook, known locally as Scuttlebrook, flowed down the centre of Leysbourne, the east end of the High Street. It formed a pool which later had to be diverted underground for road widening, where Leysbourne High Street and Church Street met. A pump on the grass verge commemorates the spot.

The Eight Bells Inn in Church Street was built in the fourteenth century for the use of the stonemasons at work on the church.

"Come through to the bar, Miss, where there's a good fire," was my friendly greeting. An old man, warming his backside, moved along for me to see the fire.

"Wicked day for sprout pickin'," he said.

"Sooner you than me, I had enough of that during the war." After that, we were off on various subjects—about thieving in the markets, the merits of Jack Russell terriers, and about education, when we were joined by a local schoolmaster who agreed that the young generation lacked the common sense we possessed.

"Like a boiling of these, some of my own, I've more than enough," offered the old man, transferring some nutty sprouts from his roomy pockets to mine as we parted in the gateway.

Beyond the Eight Bells are the almshouses, and opposite is a walled dip which when filled with water was used by carters in hot weather to soak the wooden wheels of their carts and prevent the wood from shrinking. The large cart-wheel in the museum clearly illustrates this problem, the central heating being the cause, rather than the effects of a long, dry summer.

Sir Baptist's great Campden House was burnt by the Royalists in the Civil War but the Jacobean lodges and gateway beside the path to the church give some idea of its splendour. The house is said to have cost £29,000 and was built of local stone in an ornate Italian style. It caused much adverse comment from the Campdenians, though they were grateful for the employment it brought, as times were bad, owing to the decline in the wool trade. Travellers on the wolds, too, were grateful for the light from the lantern in the glass dome of the house, which guided them to Campden.

In the churchyard, lime trees, planted originally in 1770, when the flowers were gathered for lime tea, still line the path to the church. Inside are the brasses to the Grevels and other local families. The black and white marble tomb of Sir Baptist and his wife, which cost £1,500, is considered ill suited to the church, but the exquisitely carved marble shows clearly the costumes of the period. There is a slightly humorous memorial to the Noels, as they stand, hand in hand, by an open cupboard door. Above all, do not miss the really rare fifteenth-century embroideries, so admired by Queen Mary.

I first learned of the architect F. L. Griggs and many other Cotswold artists and craftsmen from B. J. Fletcher who, on his retirement in 1928 from the post of Director of Art Education in Birmingham, lived first at Bourton-on-the-Hill and later at Daneway House at Sapperton. We walked many miles together over the Cotswolds, discussing various groups of craftsmen who had left an enduring mark on the Cotswold villages—particularly the group of architects Ernest Gimson, Ernest and Sidney Barnsley and Norman Jewson, who established themselves at Sapperton in the early 1900s. The workshops at Daneway House were made famous by them, as they employed master craftsmen in the making of furniture and fittings worthy of the houses the group was commissioned to build. Examples of their work may be seen in many places in the Cotswolds.

We discussed the work of those attracted to Campden after the Guild of Handicrafts had settled there. The Guild moved from London to Chipping Campden in 1902 and

One of the workshops in the old silk mill in Sheep Street, Chipping Campden

for their headquarters took the silk mill in Sheep Street, which had been closed since 1842. Led by C. R. Ashbee, M.A., architect, idealist and disciple of William Morris and Ruskin, the craftsmen and their families restored cottages, installed electric light at the mill—the first in Campden—settled in the town and brought new interests to the local people. The Guild attracted many other artists and craftsmen to the town, and since then Chipping Campden has remained a centre for the arts.

At the old mill, silk thread was once made for the ribbon industry at Coventry, until that industry was ruined when French ribbons were allowed into England free of tax in 1857. The Pyments, now builders, own the mill and occupy the ground floor, but their family came to Campden as craftsmen with the Guild, as did the Harts, a family of silversmiths who have their workshop on the first floor of the mill. Here the benches are strewn with all the tools of their craft, together with silver in work. The walls are covered with records of past work and drawings of the work in hand. Henry Hart and his sons, the third generation of silversmiths, have never lacked work. Hart silver graces many English churches and I was shown photographs of the beautiful rose bowl they had made as a wedding present for the Queen and of the casket given to the Duchess of Gloucester when she received the freedom of the City of Gloucester. On the wall two large maps, one of the British Isles and the other of the world, carried a mass of pins indicating the destinations of items of Hart silver, dating from the beginning of the firm.

Invited to sign the visitors' book, I felt the quality of the beautiful hand-made paper, made by members of the Guild in 1903 for Ashbee's Essex Press. Ashbee had taken over William Morris's Kelmscott presses after the death of the latter. He moved the press to Campden when the lease of Essex House, a seventeenth-century manor in the Mile End Road, expired. The visitors' book was also handsomely bound in tooled leather, with metal clasps. In it were many famous names. An American lady who had called in 1972 was convinced that she had been there before, when she was a young child, before her family left for America. One of the Harts asked for her maiden name and obligingly looked through the early entries in the book, finding her childish signature—1905. Among the famous signatures was that of Frank Lloyd Wright, the American architect, who stayed with Ashbee in 1910 on his way home from Europe.

Since the coming of the Guild, Chipping Campden has had a dramatic society. Barry Jackson performed there with his Pilgrim Players in the early 1900s, before he built the Birmingham Repertory Theatre. Various members of Campden families, including the Harts, are keen Thespians. Henry Hart's brother has been playing for many

28

years in the radio series 'The Archers', and one of the younger members of the family is an active member of the present dramatic society.

In complete contrast to the Harts' workshop are the offices and workshop of Robert Welch, on the top floor of the mill. A silversmith trained in Birmingham, London and Scandinavia, Welch took over the top floor from Alec Miller, a member of the Guild, who left for America to pursue his work as a sculptor. Robert Welch has an international reputation as a designer of domestic stainless steel, cast-iron cooking utensils and light fittings. He still designs silverware, but most of the work is carried out by John Limbrey, his assistant for many years. The neat, sparklingly white walls of his studio were lined with Bauhaus posters and photographs of modern articles in stainless steel. From the window, I looked down on the wooden sheds once used by Ashbee's Guild workers and on the cottages he repaired for them, beyond the Pyments' yard. A sign of the times in this yard was the collection of old stone rick-staddles, often cut by farm workers, who could turn their hands to most jobs. These staddles were used to keep the rats out of the timber barns which they supported; nowadays they are sought-after garden ornaments.

F. L. Griggs, R.A., was known for his watercolours and etchings, many of which are preserved in the British Museum and the Victoria and Albert Museum. He lived most of his life in Campden and died there in 1938. Much of his time and his small financial resources were given to the preservation of the town and, against opposition from many quarters, he made Campden people realize the importance of their heritage. Originally, it was Griggs who accepted the financial responsibility which saved Dover's Hill for the National Trust and there is a memorial to him on the topograph.

When admiring Campden's High Street, look up to the wrought-iron signs, especially the one over the ironmonger's, which was designed by Griggs. He also instigated the move to restore some of the buildings, such as the Old Plough Inn, The King's Arms Pantry and the ironmonger's shop, when he became a member of the National Trust Committee. The enthusiasm generated by this man still lives on, for in 1942, the Market Hall, up for sale and threatened with removal to America, was bought by the National Trust. Griggs had many artist friends; Sir Alfred Munnings stayed with him and Graham Sutherland has admitted owing much to Griggs.

Another artist connected with the Guild was the illustrator Walter Crane, whose picture book, *Flora's Feast*, gave pleasure to many children who remembered the names of the flowers from the paintings which surrounded his short hand-lettered jingles—

The steep roofs of The Martins, one of the many fine houses in the High Street, Chipping Campden

Lords and Ladies of the wood,
With shaking spear and riding hood.

In the Town Hall is the last surviving truncheon with which Sir James Fox armed his special constables against Isambard Brunel and his railway engineers, who wanted to bring the new railway into Campden, alongside Berrington Mill. It bears the cryptic inscription "1844—Defeated Isambard Brunel". After fierce opposition, headed by Lord Gainsborough (the title now held by the Noel family), the branch line from Stratford-upon-Avon was taken via Honeybourne. Thus Campden station, now closed, is a mile and a half away near Battle Bridge, and the town was saved from the sordid buildings attached to the early railways.

The Town Hall, of uncertain date, incorporates two buttresses, the only remaining parts of St Katherine's Chapel which was built in 1180 by Hugh de Gonville, Lord of the Manor of Campden at the time of the murder of Thomas à Becket. The Town Hall, like most of Campden, is a lively place. Property sales and bingo sessions are held there. The parish clerk, himself a fine caligrapher who teaches lettering at the Art School, organizes many exhibitions held at the Town Hall. Being also a heraldry enthusiast, he helped raise the money for the town's coat of arms, designed at the Royal College of Arms. What finer motto for Campden than 'History in Stone'.

I was given tea in a manor house in Paxford by one of my art school friends, many of whom have been lucky enough to settle and work in the Cotswolds. Her pottery figures have all the humour of a Daumier drawing, her silver work she learned from the Harts, but most of her time is given to the surrounding churches, where her flower arrangements with their religious themes are in great demand.

We had tea by a massive stone fireplace where the log fire blazed in a wrought-iron basket with beautiful split finials, an example of the local blacksmith's craft. I stroked the Siamese cat, which had laid the house ghost. Sad moans used to come from the large copper log-container, until one evening the cat leapt into the hod and set up such a howling that the ghostly moans were heard no more.

In spite of food shortages, hares were rarely eaten in medieval times, as they were believed to be witches in disguise. Paxford's witch died at the end of the last century, soon after the village boys had been trying to shoot a hare. They had seen it many times at dusk and one evening they were lucky and riddled it with shot as it took refuge in old Jane's garden. They searched among the vegetables and fruit bushes but never found their quarry or saw it again. When the time came for old Jane to be laid out for burial, her back was found to be covered with shot marks.

31

As I drove home in the gathering dusk, it was a fox, not a hare, which was dazzled by my headlights. I switched them off to allow him to find the hedge in peace and thought of the many times I had driven home from Campden during World War II, when all headlights were fitted with shutters. Their light would not have dazzled a mole.

Working in a rented Cotswold barn, we heard the planes going over the hills for the longed-for Normandy invasion. We rushed out of the barn to wave them good luck, as they towed their hundreds of gliders towards the coast of France. What a contrast with the invasion in the opposite direction 900 years earlier, when Hugh d'Avranches crossed the Channel in one of the small ships of his uncle, William of Normandy. It was he who, after being created Earl of Chester, was later rewarded with the manor of Chipping Campden.

The pump in Leysbourne at the corner of Church Street, marking the site of the old Scuttle-brook

CHAPTER TWO

Broad Campden to Broadway

A glimpse of the lantern on the fifteenth-century dovecote in the garden of Westington House

The road beyond the mill at Chipping Campden leads to the winding villages of Westington and Broad Campden, so different from Chipping Campden, in that the stone houses are mainly thatched.

The craft of the thatcher has declined in the last thirty years. With the present cost of labour, rethatching is an expensive business, even if an expert thatcher is available. Many owners of thatched houses have had, for financial reasons, to re-roof their properties with the new composition stone tiles—not so beautiful as the old ones, but one must in all fairness acknowledge that the manufacturers have made an exceedingly good job of the imitations. Unfortunately, moss and lichen seem reluctant to grow on them.

I was fortunate enough to be visiting the Cotswold historian Jack Nelson when the thatchers were finishing a new roof on some of the out-buildings in the Nelsons' grounds in Broad Campden. The house and out-buildings stand on three sides of a square, having been converted in the 'twenties from farm buildings. The main part of the house was an Elizabethan granary barn and at right angles on the left-hand side are the converted cart sheds, which are thatched with Norfolk reeds. The cow bowsings on the third side were covered with brushwood, a rare survival from the past. The bowsings now form a long and delightful summer-house, with a view across what was once

33

Broad Campden, which like Westington has many houses roofed with thatch

the farmyard, to the garden sides of the house. When the thatch covering had to be replaced, the thatchers, who were local men from Offenham, had to find their long-stemmed wheat straw from as far away as Devon. Modern combine harvesters rarely make long-stemmed straw available. The local thatchers had done their work well, but the cost was not much under £4,000 and the roof had taken three men ten weeks to complete.

I had called to congratulate Jack Nelson on his new book on Chipping Campden. Few historians have had the good fortune to have a domestic help who was know-ledgeable enough to rescue some old documents before they went on a bonfire. The story of how the Rushout papers from Northwick Park came into his hands makes fascinating reading.

Jack Nelson, like so many people who have the good fortune to live in a Cotswold village, devotes much of his time to helping the various preservation societies. Until his recent retirement, he was chairman of the Campden Trust and of the local branch of the National Trust. His expert knowledge of canoeing was invaluable to the Upper Avon Navigation Trust when that river was made navigable and connected, at Stratford-upon-Avon, with the Midland canal network. As a magistrate and youth club worker, he appreciated the need for local leisure ac-tivities, and as a walker, he gave his strong support to saving, opening up and signposting the many paths over the Cotswolds now readily available to walkers. He was obviously not alone in these endeavours and the casual observer should be grateful for the time gladly given by so many Cotswold residents in making the whole area such a wonderful place to visit.

The Norman chapel in Broad Campden (now a private house) was restored by C. R. Ashbee in 1905 to house his Essex House Press. In the church of St Michael, both the altar rail and the chalice were designed by him and made by his Guild of Handicrafts.

Behind the church is a small house, once the home of Jonathan Hulls, the son of a weaver farmer who was con-sidered a failure in his own time. Nowadays, he rates high among steam enthusiasts, for in 1736 he invented steam navigation. This was a remarkable achievement for a Cotswold farmer, who had had to obtain his knowledge from reading scientific journals. In his time, steam engines were used only for pumping water from mines. He re-alized that a steam engine could be used for driving a rotary paddle-wheel. Lack of money and sympathetic support prevented him from becoming as famous as James Watt, but his drawings, dated 1737, are preserved in the British Museum. A salute to his memory was given years later, when his portrait was hung in the new liner, the *Queen Mary*.

A sailing boat towed by Jonathan Hull's steam-driven paddle boat

At the other end of the village is the studio of Doris Lindner. She began by drawing animals and cutting them out in paper on the nursery floor. Later, she had the good fortune to study animal anatomy and painting at Frank Calderon's school in Kensington. There they worked with both live models and skeletons, until they knew exactly how and why every movement of an animal was made. This master craftswoman was chosen to model that great racehorse Arkle, whose bronze statue stands in the small paddock at Cheltenham, facing the famous course on which he won so many races. Examining the full-size model from which the bronze was cast, it was easy to see the immense power of the shoulder muscles and the beauty of the slender head.

Since the Royal Worcester Porcelain Company discovered her work, she has modelled for them many fine pieces now sought by collectors all over the world—the Queen, at the Trooping of the Colour, Prince Philip on a polo pony, Princess Anne taking a jump, Richard Mead on Lauriston, a Hackney, and a Clydesdale stallion. But these have been no more important to her than the prancing of a lively Welsh pony or a mare and foal, entitled 'The New-Born'. Many bronzes of her dogs have been cast for public sale, but she is never happy about modelling dogs unless she knows them well and can make drawings of their many moods. On one visit, her joyous French bulldog puppy, Henry Quizz of Quartz, met me at the gate with such pleasurable abandon I was nearly bowled back into the road. Now three and a half years old, his puppy portrait cast in bronze is on sale by Heredities.

On the way to Blockley, I took the lane which runs beside Northwick Park and stopped on the top of Campden Hill to look back at the Chipping Campden buildings,

Blockley, at one time an important centre for silk weaving

their stones glowing in the November sunlight. It is a good and peaceful place from which to view the town, with its long line of buildings in the wide valley. Enjoying the view I noticed a flock of greenfinches busy in the hedge, when suddenly, in a fllash, off they went. A golden retriever had disturbed them as he came trotting along, hurrying back to the farm with the squirrel which dangled from his jaws like a huge grey moustache.

From Donkey Lane, one of the ridge lanes above Blockley, is a view down to its long, narrow street. Fortunately for the peace of the village, this street ends in a footpath which leads up through Dovedale and Bourton Woods, and along a narrow lane up to the wolds, so that the street is bypassed by the main-road traffic. The position of this village is a complete contrast to the wide, flat site of Chipping Campden. The locals say the bowling green is the only level piece of ground. The cottages cling like limpets to the steep hillside and narrow lanes lead down to the mills on the brook below.

A bishop of Worcester bought the manor of Blockley from the Saxon overlord Burgred for 300 shillings. When sheep became a valuable asset for trading, the flocks of the bishops were driven down to Blockley for shearing and in 1384 an eight-bay sheep-cot was built there. In the fourteenth century, the bishops of Worcester had a summer palace beside the church, probably on the site of the present Manor House, which is mostly seventeenth century. At the rear of the house, the stone roof-tiles are only just above the churchyard turf, but the façade faces a terraced garden supported by an enormous wall and beyond this the garden, like so many in the village, slopes down to the brook.

The size of the church of St Peter and St Paul also indicates a large village in early times, long before the population explosion caused by the short-lived silk boom. The church building shows a variety of styles and alterations, from late Norman to the restoration in 1871. The tombs in the church commemorate the families who lived at Northwick Park—the Childes and the Rushouts, who became the Lord Northwicks.

Cars are best left at the open end of the village by the church—the streets, houses and mills can be better observed on foot.

'The Brook', a small feeder of Knee Brook, was dammed up to make some surprisingly large pools to feed the silk mills. By 1823, there were eight mills supplying the Coventry ribbon trade and giving employment to some 3,000 people, not only in the mill buildings, but also to families of out-workers in the surrounding farms and cottages. This industry was developed by the Rushout family, who had bought nearby Northwick Park in 1683. They had financial interests in the Dutch East India Company and the Levant Company and they gave generously to help the Huguenot Society. This is why many foreign silk workers, mostly Flemish, found work in Blockley.

The industry positively boomed, until the removal in 1860 of the protective duty levied on imported silk, which ruined many of the Coventry weavers. By 1880, when William Morris came to Blockley looking for a workshop, his companion, the tile-maker William de Morgan, wrote: "The mills were all empty . . . so many people out of work." Unfortunately for the unemployed, much as Morris loved the village, he and de Morgan chose a site nearer to London for their pottery. Many workers had to leave the village and the deserted mills eventually became dilapidated. They have since been restored and are used, one of them as a waterworks and the others as private houses. I spent several holidays at one of Blockley's mills during World War II and since then, apart from some new cottages on one of the ridge lanes, little has changed.

A feeder of the brook comes down the hillside by Dovedale Woods, through the garden of Fish Cottage, where a trout is hand fed in a small pool beside the tombstone of an old fish aged twenty years, which died in 1855. Along the street the winter jasmine was in full flower and the red valerian, which grows like a weed between the warm stones, was still in summer bloom. Blockley is a favourite haunt of the pied wagtail and they were bobbing about from one garden to another. One main-street footpath is well above the road, and alleyways lead via further steep flights of steps to the cottages above. In a studio, some friends were working in stained glass. Just completed was a small memorial window for Blockley church, the design embodying the spirit of the Cotswolds, the hills, the woods, the stone buildings, the sheep and some of the wild flowers. It is to the memory of an American who had loved to spend his holidays walking over the wolds and the memorial is now in the church.

Further along the street, the Bell Inn was recently converted into flats and, under the floor of the public bar, nine skeletons were found. At first, some early massacre was suspected, but one of the skeletons, which was over seven feet in height and known locally as 'Long John', was found to date to approximately A.D. 840.

Among the houses in the High Street, mainly eighteenth or early nineteenth century, is one charming house with a date-stone of 1732. Its bowed windows are in complete harmony with the stone façade. Opposite is the studio of a young sculptor who works in wood, stone and fibreglass and delights in making wooden models for children. These are beautifully carved and turned, each a collector's piece. In his spare time, he was working on a doll's house, an amusing semi-circular Emmett-like construction, with prancing seahorses forming balustrades and clowns' heads the catches to a secret room. The ground floor was eventually to become a toy shop but the whole conception was full of surprises. This, his hobby, is a complete change from his serious business, which is the making of fibreglass mouldings, such as oast-house cowls and large sculptured pieces in wood or fibreglass for public buildings:

The blackened ruins of Rock Cottage have been derelict for many years and only recently has a daring young architect begun to rebuild it. According to the neighbours, that house has a 'hoodoo' upon it, in that owners after Joanna Southcott died have been affected in strange ways. Joanna was a world-famed prophetess in her day (1750–1814). At an early age, she claimed to have "a still small voice speaking within". She made thousands of prophecies and in 1807 her Believers numbered at least 14,000. Bishops complained that their flocks were straying after Joanna. For the last ten years of her life, she poured out her prophecies and was consulted at Rock Cottage by many famous people, including the Prince Regent.

The time came for her, at the age of sixty, to give birth to the holy child Shiloh. It was then thought proper for her to take unto herself a Joseph—an obliging Mr Smith of Blockley, one of her Believers. She was reported to have died in childbirth, but the child was taken to Heaven before being seen by mortal man. Her faithful biographer

became mentally disturbed, and unfit to live alone at Rock Cottage, a companion was found for her. After the biographer's death, the companion stayed on at Rock Cottage, but the place had a strange effect on her. She took to flinging paraffin on the log fires to kill the faces she saw therein, until eventually, both she and the cottage went up in flames.

The British Museum holds a collection of Joanna Southcott's writings and there is a portrait of her in the National Portrait Gallery which is entitled 'The Prophetess'.

Along the lane from Blockley stands the mansion in Northwick Park. Built about 1686 and altered in 1732 for Sir John Rushout from designs by Lord Burlington, a picture gallery was added in 1832. Occasionally during World War II, this was opened to the public who came to enjoy Captain Spencer-Churchill's famous collection of pictures. The money raised went towards the upkeep of a camp for Polish refugees which the Captain had established in the park. It was he who first provided electric light for the village of Blockley and for his own house, the power being generated from one of his water mills. After his death, the pictures were sold and the estate was purchased by Lord Cowdray.

For some years, the house was rented to the Rev. Frank Wilson's world-wide organization, 'Life for the World', whose work is devoted to the rehabilitation of young drug addicts. To the limit of the money at their disposal, the house was partially restored, centrally heated and furnished in spartan fashion—an echoing hollow mockery of its former grandeur. The empty picture gallery was used for five-a-side football; the stables housed large, electrically driven printing presses which poured out literature for the organization, which now has an office in Blockley and a girls' hostel in Broadway. The young men at Northwick are shortly to be moved to a smaller house in Hertfordshire and the future of the house is undecided. The fate of this effort by 'Life of the World' is depressing. So much money has been given by well-wishers and by the State for young people who, as one of them explained, "prefer to live on a happy cloud and die at 25, rather than face a possible 75 years of responsibility, tax payment and boring unemployment".

The winds on Upton Wold high above Blockley soon dispersed my depression. The archaeologists have been able to work on the Wold and have a plan of the village which was abandoned in the fourteenth century. They found an example of a thirteenth-century farmhouse, typical of those in the mountainous parts of Britain, with the dwelling and the byre all under one roof. The abandonment of this village may have been due to the Black Death, or to the greed of the bishops, who enclosed much of the land on the Cotswolds for the grazing of their large and profitable flocks of sheep, thereby destroying the livelihood of many humble smallholders. Sir Thomas More, writing about enclosures in his *Utopia*, observed: "Your sheep, that were wont to be so meek and tame and so small eaters, now, as I hear say, be become so great devourers and so wild, that they eat up and swallow down, the very men themselves." For those interested in ancient farming methods, there are fine examples of ridge and furrow ploughing still to be seen from the hills above Blockley, looking down towards Lower Ditchford.

Many good walks lead out of Blockley, one over Blockley Downs to the lanes round Batsford Park, and a steeper one which leads to Upton Wold. A more sheltered gentle walk is the one up the Dovedale which skirts the edge of Bourton Woods, offering peace and silence under the trees and a variety of birds, butterflies and wild flowers.

I have driven over the Cotswold hills many times, to introduce foreign friends to their beauty. One of the most rewarding and lively of these trips was in 1947. I was one of the guides who escorted some of the American company playing 'Oklahoma' at Drury Lane. After a reception at the theatre at Stratford-upon-Avon, we made for the hills. It was a sunny Sunday, our visitors were young, unsophisticated and full of wonder at all they saw, so dif-

Broadway, the Lygon Arms. In 1251 the lord of the manor established a market by the ancient drovers' track known as The Broad Way

ferent from today's tourists, rushing round Europe in a week, with barely time to click their cameras and buy their souvenirs. We showed our guests the view of thirteen counties (this was before the recent boundary alterations), from the Tower on Broadway Beacon, at the top of Fish Hill, over 1,000 feet above sea level. This tower was a folly, built in the eighteenth century by the Earl of Coventry as an eye-catcher from his home, Croom Court in Worcestershire. We told them how Burne-Jones, William Morris and Rossetti had enjoyed spending their summers in the tower until their turn came to carry the groceries 600 feet up Fish Hill.

Today, the 55-foot tower is one of the features of the Broadway Tower Country Park. The four-storey tower houses an observation room and an exhibition of costumes and furniture in use about 1800. With three costumed figures beside the small dining table, there is little room to move and it is not surprising the Pre-Raphaelite tenants got on each other's nerves in such cramped living quarters.

The country park is extremely well laid out, with a natural history section in the 150-year-old Tower Barn. The aim of the centre is to provide information about all aspects of the wild life and plants of the countryside. The views are magnificent, the car parks ample, and information leaflets and refreshments are available.

On the occasion of the visit of our Americans, we saw the full beauty of Broadway's stone buildings as we drove slowly down Fish Hill to the melodious strains of Rogers and Hammerstein's song—

Oh what a beautiful day . . .
Everythin's goin' my way.

We walked down the wide street, a Broad Way long before the present stone houses added to its beauty. It was one of the ancient routes from the high wolds to the valley of the Severn and the port of Bristol. With a few exceptions building began in Shakespeare's time and has continued since then, with a variety of architecture.

The coaching era brought new life to the quiet farming community and at that time, the village had twenty-three inns. The White Hart was the most important for several hundred years. In 1830, the estate on which the inn stood was purchased by General Lygon, who had fought at Waterloo and had retired to Spring Hill. Here he amused himself by having clumps of beech trees planted in the grounds, following as closely as possible the dispositions of the main bodies of the troops at the Battle of Waterloo. His far-sighted butler was more realistic and saw the business potential of the White Hart, eventually persuading the general to sell it to him. He renamed it the Lygon

43

Arms and was allowed to use the family coat of arms on the sign. But it was Sydney Bolton Russell, one of the first of the English hoteliers, who was responsible for the world-renowned hotel of today. He bought the premises in 1904 and decided to restore the building and build up an antique business in order to fill it with furniture suited to the various period rooms.

When the coaching business declined with the advent of the railways, many of the old houses and cottages became dilapidated, until Broadway was discovered by the intellectuals of the 1890s, who moved in and restored them. The village attracted the artists J. S. Sargeant and Laurence Alma-Tadema, the writers J. M. Barrie and Robert Hichens, and the composers Vaughan Williams and Edward Elgar. William Morris recommended it to his friends E. A. Abbey and Frank Millet, and when the American actress Madame de Navarro retired to Broadway, she and her husband converted the two houses which became their home and their wide circle of friends adopted Broadway. Among them was Phil May, the *Punch* artist, who caricatured them all.

Since those days, with the coming of the motor car, the beauty of the village has attracted thousands of people. The poet Michael Drayton wrote about tourism at the end of the sixteenth century:

How many paltry, foolish, painted things,
That now in coaches trouble every street.

but in 1947, tourism had not taken over in Broadway and the cottages were not converted into tea, souvenir and antique shops; ours were the only cars in the wide street.

We saw the old church of St Eadburgha, with its brasses of the Dastons, a family connected with the Sheldons, the last great landowners of Broadway, who lived at the Manor House beside the church. In the church is a rather indecipherable memorial to one of its benefactors, Sir Thomas Phillips. He was the son of a local family of tradesmen and farmers who had lived in Broadway for several generations. He inherited his father's estate at Middle Hill and indulged his passion for collecting books. His eccentric ambition was to have, "one copy of every book in the world". The rooms at Middle Hill became piled high with books and there was little space left for eating or sleeping. He died in 1872 and his library is still being sold.

We took the field path behind St Eadburgha's to Buckland—"the land held by book", once part of the monastic lands of Gloucester Abbey. When the path leaves the woods, there is a splendid view of the church of St Michael, the manor house and rectory in the valley below. The churchyard may be entered from a door in the manor garden wall, thus giving an excellent view of the

Buckland, a small hamlet near Broadway

frontage of this fine sixteenth-century house. St Michael's was a possession of the Abbey of Gloucester from the thirteenth century to the Dissolution. The only loss in the careful restoration in 1885 was the medieval frescoes; the fifteenth-century encaustic tiles were carefully copied. Three panels of stained glass, dated by the lady's costume to about 1475, were restored by William Morris at his own expense. Many of the oak bench-pews are fifteenth century and the oak panelling in the aisles, complete with hat pegs, was given in 1615. The carved stonework, although mutilated, is thought to have been brought from Hailes Abbey after the Dissolution. The beautifully embroidered blue velvet cope, also from Hailes, is thought to have been worn by William Whychurch, Abbot of Hailes in 1464–79.

We were kindly allowed to show our overseas guests the impressive hall in the oldest medieval parsonage house in the country. It is open to the public during normal weekday visiting hours. As we left the village, a flock of white fantails flew out from their perches on the square church tower and its stone angels trumpeted us a silent farewell.

Our guests sang more songs for us and we all wished we had a "surrey with a fringe on top" to save us the walk back to Broadway to the hospitality of the Lygon Arms, where the ladies quickly accepted an invitation to be shown over the famous bedrooms in this historic old house.

Adjoining the Lygon Arms are the showrooms and workshops of Gordon Russell, son of S. B. Russell. After his return from World War I, he decided to leave his father's hotel business and the repairing of old furniture, and design and make first-class contemporary furniture. He used to expound his views on design to the then newly formed Design in Industry Association, of which I was an enthusiastic member. He purchased the premises next door to the Lygon Arms and so began the Gordon Russell workshops, where great emphasis was placed on quality of material, design and workmanship. A new era in English furniture began. His early pieces showed the influence of Ernest Gimson and the Barnsley brothers of the Sapperton group and were made of the less familiar English woods, cherry, yew, laburnum and holly. They were polished but unstained, allowing the full beauty of the natural colour of the wood to be revealed. Examples of this furniture of the 1920s have been selected as the nucleus of a museum in the present showrooms of Gordon Russell Contracts Ltd. One of the most beautiful specimens is a chest of drawers in holly wood, as supplied to Lloyd George. The handles were made by Henry Gardiner, a metal worker for Ernest Gimson and employed by Gordon Russell after Gimson's death in 1919. Gardiner could make anything in metal, having learned the hard way, in what he called "the dog holes of Birmingham", where he worked as a locksmith and gunsmith. Although the handles on this holly-wood chest appear at a casual glance to be of steel, they are wrought in rustless iron, which forges more successfully than steel.

The large mechanized workshops of the 1970s, making first-class furniture for home and export markets, stand discreetly hidden behind the original workshops, which are now used as showrooms. In spite of mass production, with chairs made by the thousand to reseat our great cathedrals, there is still the same pride and enthuasiasm for first-class workmanship. I was shown round by one of the young designers of the firm, himself a fine craftsman in turned wood. The foreman, with obvious pride, allowed me to see a drawing of the beautiful chairs made for Princess Anne, chairs with a spindle back combining the initials M and A.

The Gordon Russell export drive is vigorous, and designs of furniture licensed to be made in Japan are carefully supervised. They also have developed an expanding market in the Arabian Gulf, where there is a great potential demand for high-quality furniture.

In addition to large concerns like the Russells, there are in many of the villages, artists, and craftsmen who, in the same way as the medieval sheep farmers, are concerned with foreign markets in addition to work for their own communities.

From the showrooms in Broadway, I went to talk with Sir Gordon Russell at his home on the side of Dover's Hill, a house with wide views of Chipping Campden in the valley below and of the distant hills beyond. He now spends his time as a design consultant, having retired from his post as Director of the Council of Industrial Design. He commented on modern design in building, the new housing estates which are spreading around the larger Cotswold villages, emphasizing the excellent one at Chipping Campden, the less happy examples at Mickleton and the regrettable red roofs beside the approach road to Broad Campden. He told me of the work involved in the development of the Broadway Country Park which he, in conjunction with local societies, had established and of the interesting details of the topograph. This was designed and constructed in the Bryant Fedden workshop at Winchcombe. The map, four feet in diameter, indicates the four points of the compass, and a number of places from New York to Broadway. It was erected to the memory of his brother Don Russell, a former chairman of the planning committee. After talking about various friends and pioneers of the original Design in Industries Association and its ultimate development in the Design Centre in the Haymarket, London, we walked in the garden.

From there it is possible to see how well the house, begun in 1924 and built in true Cotswold tradition, fits in with the steep hillside. The retaining walls are the problem in any hillside garden. His most recent one, built with hundreds of tons of local stone, was constructed by Sir Gordon himself. "Modern bricklayers, who were the only help I could get, don't understand stone," he explained. He showed me his various experiments with concrete—interesting textures made with corrugated paper, wattle and water-lily leaves impressed into the surface, and walls made of railway sleepers thinly coated with concrete, the rough knotted texture of the wood clearly visible. He was not so happy about some columns in which he had left nesting holes.

"So far, I have had no tenants and I don't know how one advertises. I've tried all the usual bait of suet and nuts. Now that chap is different, he thinks I come into the garden purely for his benefit!"

"That chap" was a robin, which had appeared immediately we stepped out on to the terrace to examine the fossils in a polished table-top of Derbyshire stone. He followed us round the garden, chirping loudly at every stop because the boss had forgotten his bag of crumbs.

Examining pieces of Sir Gordon's carving, we talked of the early Cotswold masons, whose date-stones were mostly carved for their own pleasure—an extra flourish to finish off a good façade, always right in size and proportion, because they knew exactly where they were to be placed. So many modern pieces ordered by architects may often be more skilfully carved, yet do not relate to their site, which the stonemason has probably never seen. Sir Gordon had carved a headstone for an archway leading from a long flight of steps down the side of the terrace. It was large—five feet in length. Placing it in position without any lifting gear had been a major problem. In the end, he said, "We became like the savages described by Dr Johnson on his tour of Scotland. What we lacked in brains we made up for in patience. We had to move the stone on wooden rollers along the entire length of the wall."

Patience has been the keynote of all his work in the garden, which is visited by a great variety of birds because of the water which flows down either side of the long flight of stone steps, to a canal on the bottom terrace, which has a back retaining wall of bottle-glass arches. The small cyclamen and all the varieties of hellebores, so difficult to grow in a town garden, were spreading prolifically under the fruit trees together with the primroses and snowdrops—a garden worthy of this skilful designer and craftsman.

"Forgetful though!" chirped the robin, determined to have the last word.

Broadway, looking towards Fish Hill and the Broadway Country Park

The gateway of Stanway House. Was it designed by Inigo Jones or by
Timothy Strong, a Cotswold mason?

CHAPTER THREE

Stanton to Naunton

The Cotswold Way passes above Buckland by the old quarry workings at No Man's Land, up to the Iron Age hillfort at Shenberrow and down into Stanton and Stanway.

Mrs Mary Delany, famous for her *Memoirs* and also for her portrait by Opie in the National Gallery, lived at Buckland. The tombs of her father, Colonel Bernard Granville (1725), and his wife are in Buckland churchyard. The young Mary Granville's best friend was Sarah Kirkham at Stanton and on most days these two walked over the hills to visit one another.

John Wesley also trod the local walks when he came down from Oxford to stay with his many friends around Broadway. He stayed at Buckland Rectory for Sarah Kirkham's wedding and preached at the Sunday morning service at Buckland during the Christmas holiday, walking across to Stanton to preach there in the afternoon. A walk over the hills, starting either from Buckland or Snowshill, brings you to the top of Stanton's cul-de-sac street and to The Mount Inn, a good place to rest and look down on the village of Stanton and the farms on the rising hill opposite.

Higher up the hill, approached through the car park of The Mount Inn, a steep path leads up to the Stanton Guildhouse. This was started in 1963 to provide a centre for a creative way of living. There are classes for local groups from October to May and some residential courses in the summer months. All aspects of the craft of weaving are already well established and classes for woodwork, wrought iron and stone work are to follow as the buildings are completed. Many of the tutors are well-known Cotswold artists and craftsmen who give their time voluntarily. Art exhibitions, musical evenings and serious discussion groups are well attended, confirming the need for this type of centre. The building labour was provided by student volunteers and this is a tribute in stone to present-day craftsmanship. The site is superb, high above the village, and commanding even wider views than those from The Mount.

Stanton is a quiet village with no tourist attractions other than the beauty of its weathered stone buildings and well-kept gardens, but it was not always thus. It has suffered many adversities, and at one period the properties

Stanton's medieval cross with seventeenth-century sundial and globe

Walking down this street, I was followed by a gaggle of inquisitive Chinese geese, with their long, brown-striped necks at full stretch, until I turned at the medieval cross to walk up the passage to the church. This is small, part Norman, with traces of early fourteenth-century wall paintings. Many Cotswold churches were used during the Civil War to house prisoners, and this in most cases resulted in severe damage to the buildings. Much beautiful wood carving was used as firewood, for heating and for cooking, and many windows were smashed as a result of frustration and boredom. The east window of St Michael's was destroyed—the fifteenth-century glass figures now in the window came from Hailes Abbey and were reset in modern glass by Sir Ninian Comper as a war memorial after World War I.

Tombs of three local families are in the church, the Izods, the Wynniates and the Warrens. The Izods came originally from Chapel Izod, County Kilkenny, about 1450, settling near Chipping Campden. This family built Stanton Court during the reign of James I. The gardens, occasionally open to the public, show the knowledge and loving care of generations of good gardeners; the small brook flowing through the gardens has been used to great advantage. The property passed to the Wynniate family in the seventeenth century. Warren House was the original manor house and is older than The Court. The date-stone

were almost dilapidated. Many of the buildings owe their present good condition to Sir Philip Stott, an architect who acquired the estate in 1906 and, until his death in 1937, spent much of his time and money on the restoration of many houses and cottages, in addition to giving the village a water supply. Several reminders of this first water supply are to be seen in taps set in stone niches in the walls of the street.

'T.W.1557' refers to a portion added by Thomas Warren.

An ancient wooden carving in the church, said to be one of the original roof bosses, shows a bird surrounded by a large circle of intricate lettering in flowing ribbons, forming the name 'Maurice Wraybury'. The collection box in the wall has been set in modern carved stone, with two dolphins above the box and embossed crosses beneath.

The present street of well-kept houses and cottages shows nothing of the struggle for existence which went on in the past—the spinning, weaving and hose-making, which in the mid-seventeenth century amounted to thousands of pairs of hose each year. The villagers of those days must have slaved hard to help produce these quantities, when you consider the home baking, cheese making and all the daily household chores, with few mechanical aids. It was a struggle to pay the heavy Hearth Tax imposed by Charles II in 1622, which produced £200,000 per annum. The village also suffered the severe epidemic of fever, recorded by Dr Dover. This Dr Dover, as famous in his day as his grandfather, the 'Olimpick' Robert Dover, was known as 'Quicksilver Dover'. He had spent much of his life as a doctor on privateers and cured many sailors of the plague. He is reputed to have rescued Alexander Selkirk, the original Robinson Crusoe, from the island of Juan Fernandez in 1708. When he retired from the sea, he invented 'Dover's Powder', which, up to the beginning of this century, was sold as a sedative. He retired, an elderly widower, to live with his friend Robert Tracey at Stanway House, where he wrote his book, *The Physician's Legacy*. In this he records the fatal epidemic fever which ravaged the Cotswold villages in 1728 and killed many of the inhabitants of the farms and cottages around Stanton and Stanway.

A pleasant housing estate has been built at the lower end of the village, married into the older buildings by the conversion of large barns into cottages. Continuing, the road bends to the right, affording a pleasant drive through park land until you reach the great tithe barn beside Stanway House. For 800 years before the Dissolution, the manor belonged to the Abbey of Tewkesbury. The tithe barn was built for the abbot in the fourteenth century and still retains its two tiers of massive wind braces. The roof tile-stones, also fourteenth century, were brought from a quarry in Roman Buckle Street. The small stone doorway with a scratch dial cut into the jamb is thought to have been inserted from an earlier building. The barn was repaired in 1925 and is now well used as a village hall and theatre, which is open to the general public.

Many acres of abbey lands in the Cotswolds were acquired by wealthy Tudors after the Dissolution. The manor of Stanway was bought by the Traceys of

Toddington. Sir Paul Tracey built the present mansion about 1600. For the best view of the famous gateway to the house, walk along the lane which leads down from the Snowshill—Stumps Cross road, which runs along the top of the hill. The lane is easy to find because of the unusual war memorial on the corner, which is the work of three distinguished men. The plinth is by Sir Philip Stott, with an outstanding bronze of St George and the Dragon by Alexander Fisher, and the perfect lettering is by Eric Gill. It seems a pity that such an arresting monument, which causes many visitors to stop, should have no plaque to indicate this.

As you walk down the lane, the gateway is at the bottom of the hill, with Stanway House appearing almost too close behind it. One wonders why the gateway was placed here in the hollow, crowded against the house, and not at the entrance on the road which runs through the park. It has been an object of architectural controversy for many years. It is thought to have been built about 1630 as the customary adjunct to a Tudor mansion. The design has been attributed to Inigo Jones, though there is a more reliable theory that it was the work of Timothy Strong, the arms and the date being a later addition. Strong was one of the Cotswold master masons who leased the Taynton quarry in 1617. The stone pyramid which stands high up in the hillside garden was built by Robert Tracey in memory of his father in 1750.

The small group of houses in the hollow by the high stone wall of Stanway House stands beside the original 'Stone Way', which is a steep walk up to the ridge and across the wolds. For a more gentle approach to Snowshill, there is the 'Ladies' Road' from Stanton to Shenberrow Camp, with its easy gradient, thoughtfully provided by Sir Philip Stott.

The views from Shenberrow Hill are superb and from this point there are several tracks leading to Snowshill. Like Stanton, the Manor of Snowshill belonged to Winchcombe Abbey until the Dissolution, when Henry VIII gave both to his Queen, Catherine Parr.

The barrow at Snowshill has almost disappeared, but many objects were found there at the end of the nineteenth century. Perhaps the most famous of these is the Snowshill Dagger, now in the British Museum.

Not so famous is the Snowshill Sewing Machine, made in 1842 by Charles (or, as the villagers called him, 'Schemer') Keyte. The principle of the modern sewing machine was evolved from his idea, though not from his cumbersome machine, now on view in the Textile Machinery Gallery at the Science Museum.

Visitors today are mainly attracted to Snowshill to visit the Manor, a National Trust property. Like the museum at Chipping Campden, the house contains a most extra-

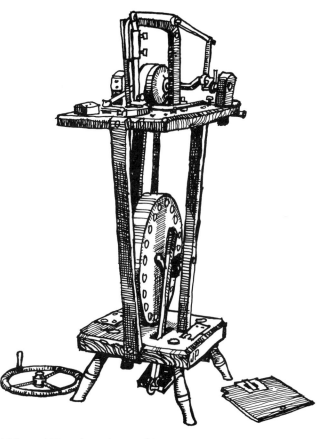

'Schemer' Keyte's sewing machine

ordinary magpie collection of objects, amassed by an eccentric owner, Charles Paget Wade. The building is a typical Cotswold manor of the early sixteenth century, with seventeenth- and eighteenth-century alterations. It was restored about 1919, when the terraced gardens were laid out. The separate small building, which has a spiral stone staircase, may have been a priest's house when the manor was a farmhouse. The whole estate is interesting and it is an opportunity to see the inside of the Manor, with its good staircases and panelled rooms. The village is a hill village, with many ancient stone cottages; the church however was rebuilt in 1864.

The surrounding country is open and windswept, equally good for walking, riding or driving, and popular with hares. I walked behind one of them, lolloping along in the road until, in one bound, it leaped the drystone wall and disappeared from view. On another occasion, while sitting quietly in the shelter of a hedge, out of the March winds, I saw eight of them, playing, chasing and boxing, like true 'mad March hares'.

There is a walk down the hill to Taddington, which was once an early settlement and has a large tithe barn, dated 1632. The Norman window and the scratch dials suggest that it may have been part of a chapel. Its beauty is now marred by the large corrugated iron structure hitched on to it. Another pleasant walk from Snowshill goes across

55

Snowshill, a typical Cotswold hill village, with many ancient stone cottages

Bourton Downs to Bourton on the Hill, where the great stone barn in the grounds of Bourton House is considered one of the finest in the Cotswolds. It is certainly one of the largest barns in the district; the date-stone shows 1570 and the initials 'R.P.' refer to Richard Palmer. It is clearly visible from the road, beautifully sited and restored, and on request visitors are allowed to see the interior.

Two of the treasures in Bourton's small church of St Laurence are a Winchester Bushel and a Winchester Peck, standard measures and so named because they were kept in the Town Hall at Winchester. One is recorded in the reign of Henry VII and it was approved as a standard measure for the whole kingdom in the reign of Elizabeth I. Bourton's bushel measure was not ordered by the local magistrates until 1816 and since the standard British bushel was introduced in 1826, it had a very short life. The Winchester measures were abolished in the reign of William IV.

A good walk from Bourton starts from the old quarries on the top of the hill, skirts Batsford Park to Cadley Hill, crosses the Downs to Blockley and returns up the Dovedale and through Bourton Woods.

One of Bourton's famous men was Sir Thomas Overbury, son of Nicholas Overbury of Bourton, poet and essayist at the court of James I. His work found no favour until, wrongly accused, he was imprisoned in the Tower

Bourton on the Hill. The church of St Laurence

and then poisoned; his poisoners were subsequently tried and hanged. After this, his poem 'The Wife', which had first brought him into disfavour, was acclaimed and made six editions in the year 1614, greatly pleasing the people of Bourton.

From the bar window of the Horse and Groom, there is a long view across the village to Moreton-in-Marsh and over to Barton-on-the-Heath, the home of Robert Dover.

The steep hill village of Bourton on the Hill is a very different place from Bourton on the Water, which lies off the Fosse Way, along the banks of the River Windrush. Outside the crowded tourist season, normal village life goes on and the River Windrush, enhanced by its low stone bridges, dating from 1775, flows serenely along its man-made bed beside the village street. For archaeologists, Bourton on the Water has an exceptional continuity as a settlement. Evidence suggests that people lived there from Neolithic times, and at Salmonsbury Camp to the east of the village there is an Iron Age fort, inhabited into Roman times. The Romano-British and Saxon villages followed, giving an unbroken history of human habitation for nearly 6,000 years. At various excavations, foundations of circular huts, a hoard of currency bars, Iron Age pottery and the site of an Anglo-Saxon hut have been found. In this hut, remains of a seventh-century upright loom, weights and pottery were discovered.

On the Fosse Way, there was a bridge in Roman times, a ford in the eighth century and another stone bridge in 1483. This last was rebuilt as a county bridge in 1806 and widened in 1961, when a plaque was added bearing a carved capricorn, the badge of the Roman Second Legion, builders of this length of Fosse Way. Most of the coins, glass and jewellery found in and around the present village date from the first to the fourth centuries. Near the original bridge, now named Bourton Bridge, is Leadenwell, home of the bird artist Paul Nicholas. When the foundations for his bungalow were excavated, a Roman well lined with lead was discovered, in such excellent condition it has been preserved in the Cheltenham Museum. Paul Nicholas's meticulous paintings of birds are on sale in Bourton's Wild Life Art Gallery at Birdland.

Like Topsy, Birdland just growed. Leonard Hill spent his boyhood caring for the birds he loved. As a builder, restoring old Cotswold buildings, he was able in 1956 to realize his life's ambition. He purchased Chardwar, a spacious sixteenth-century manor house with $3\frac{1}{2}$ acres of garden, restored the house, and in the garden built accommodation for his birds, to harmonize perfectly with the house.

Finding him in order to talk to him about his birds was like following a typhoon. "Over in the corner by the penguins"—"Just left to see to a sick flamingo"—"You've missed him by a minute, he went into the Tropical House"—"He's gone over to the house," said various members of the staff. At last I might track him down as it was morning coffee-time. "He's been here, but no time for coffee. He knocked down that pile of washing as he rushed out. Try the office."

The office is above the Wild Life Art Gallery and adjoins a large lecture hall Leonard Hill has built—there I trapped him. Talking about his birds, time was forgotten.

Bourton on the Water and the River Windrush

One of his greatest achievements is the breeding of Hahn's Macaws. It took twelve months of patient study to find the correct heat and diet required and it was four years before chicks were reared. These macaws had been extinct in Trinidad for fifty years, yet now, chicks are sent there each year and are nesting in the island again.

A walk round the Model Village (a perfect miniature of Bourton), sited in the garden of the old New Inn, is an excellent way of seeing the village as a whole, prior to your own exploration. The church is one of the few examples in the Cotswolds where the Norman church on Saxon foundations was completely demolished. The present building is largely eighteenth century. The chancel roof was painted in 1928 by T. E. Howard and carries the arms of the Abbey of Evesham, also of various people connected with the history of the parish.

Many of the houses on either side of the Windrush are good examples of Cotswold building. Boxbush House, seventeenth century, Dial House, date-signed 1698, the Old Manse, 1748, and Harrington House, perhaps the most splendid in the village, are all worth seeing. The last, restored around 1700, is now one of the Holiday Fellowship centres. Over all these beautiful buildings, many of Leonard Hill's birds fly free, though not the mischievous macaws, which developed a passion for stealing clothes pegs. Until their flights were stopped, no line of washing in the village was safe—and do not drop your car keys while walking through Birdland; the birds are tame and mingle with the visitors. My own keys were kindly picked up for me by a macaw, but before I could accept them, they were playfully tossed into the ducks' pond. Macaws resemble humans in many ways—some have a life span of eighty years and like many old people, hate to be left alone. If they are lonely, they can become neurotic and pluck out their plumage, but there is no chance of that at Birdland; it is a happy, companionable place for both birds and humans.

Before the days of insecticides, wasps used to nest in the banks of the Windrush and come in their thousands to plague the local inhabitants. Bourton on the Water, like most of the Cotswold villages, has a cricket team. On one occasion, the team had no sooner sat down in the luncheon tent than they were invaded by a swarm of wasps. Trousers were tucked into boots, shirt buttons fastened, but it was a toss-up who feasted best, until the tent blew down. Then it became a free-for-all amongst the scattered tables, heavily laden with the best village fare, wasps and cricketers alike struggling on the floor to find a way out and yet take with them some of the succulent feast.

A lady in Bourton gave me a home-made wine recipe, remarking "There's nothing like a scum of fermented woppies to give your wine a real good flavour."

There is an area of quiet Cotswold country south of Bourton, within a triangle made by three main roads. For Clapton-on-the-Hill, cross the road bridge at the end of Sherborne Street and avoid the Fosse Way, now the busy A429. The church of St James at Clapton, as a chapelry of Bourton on the Water, was an early possession of Evesham Abbey. Most of the building is late twelfth century and this is one of the smallest of the Cotswold churches. A few seventeenth-century farms cluster round the church, and one of the large barns, built from locally quarried stone, has an exterior staircase. The Clapton estate was regarded as a manor by 1620, hence the name of Manor Farm. From Upper Farmhouse (1790) there are extensive views on all sides. In Farmington Lane, the tall hedgerows were smothered with 'Old Man's Beard', sparkling white with frost. On the green in Farmington village is an octagonal pump-house on wooden struts, with eight gables and a small cupola. The new stone roof was presented to this English village by the citizens of Farmington, Connecticut, U.S.A., in 1935, to commemorate the 300th anniversary of the founding of the State of Connecticut. There are many items of interest in the Norman church, well restored with stone from the local quarry, high on the wolds above the village, with its working entrance on the Fosse Way. Good freestone is still quarried there and the dressed stone is in demand for restoration work, especially windows and lintels.

For the two large mansions in the valley, at Great Barrington and Sherborne, the stone came from the Taynton quarry near Burford and the roof tiles from the mines at Stonefield, a small village north-west of the grounds of Blenheim Palace. After the harvest and winter sowing work were completed, Stonefield men could then be spared to mine the stone, soak it in water and bury it under earth to await the frosts, when the stones were spread out to be well frosted and ready for splitting. According to the historian Dr Plot, the mine was in existence in the sixteenth century. The work was hard and poorly paid and the mine closed in 1909.

A local smith has made an ingenious churchyard gate for St Peter's, Farmington, using old horse shoes—an idea copied for the church of St James at Clapton.

The drive along the Farmington lane to Sherborne is beautiful in any season. The hills rise on the one side and Sherborne Brook winds its way through the trees on the other, widening into a lake where tons of gravel were removed for the construction of Avonmouth Dock. There was a pair of swans on the lake, but their four fully grown cygnets were flying up and down the meadows beyond the weir, obviously preparing to leave home and find their own territories.

St Mary Magdalene's Church is in Sherborne Park

Farmington. The pumphouse on the village green

and is joined to Sherborne House by a corridor. The monuments in the church to the Dutton family are the fine work of Richard Westmacott the Elder, signed and dated 1791, others, by Z. M. Rysbrack, 1749. The site of Sherborne House belonged to the Abbey at Winchcombe during the wool boom. It was bought by Thomas Dutton in 1551. On its west elevation, the original house he built has escaped the many alterations. James Dutton built the stables and coach-house in the eighteenth century, when the octagonal dovecote was moved into the stableyard.

The present Sherborne House, like Northwick Park, appears too large for our generation of private householders and it is hoped it may be purchased by the Beshara School of Intensive Esoteric Education. They will continue to have quarters at Swyre Farm but a building as large as Sherborne House would enable the group to hold residential courses.

Lodge Park, to the south-west, was built by John Dutton, 1598–1657. He was a friend of Thomas Cromwell, through whom he purchased the land for the surrounding deer park, which he was allowed to stock with bucks and does from Wychwood Forest. The house, originally a small one, was used as a grandstand, to view the coursing of the deer by greyhounds. During the season of the Bibury races, held on the neighbouring wolds, gentlemen could try out their dogs in the park on payment of 2s. 6d. per day.

Sherborne village, known to Morris Dancers by Cecil Sharp's revival of 'The Sherborne Jig', sprawls along the brook on either side of Sherborne Park. At the east end by Stone Farmhouse, cottage No. 88 incorporates the remains of an original Norman church of which one doorway can be seen from the road.

As Laurie Lee advises, sitting quietly in the country is the best way to see what wild life is about.

> Through trunks of black alder
> Runs a fox like a lantern.

He came out of a copse on the far side of the field, trotted along by the side of a hedge, then stopped and looked up. Barely visible on one of the fence posts was a small brown owl, apparently uninterested, as the fox trotted purposefully on his way, out of sight. A hare came next, skippity-hopping first this way and then that and, shortly after, two brace of pheasants came to seek their lunch amongst the winter wheat in the stony field; overhead, a hawk hovered, almost stationary.

At Windrush, there is a bridle path to the weirs and the mill. The latter is a private house, but the right of way goes between the mill and the outhouses and crosses a

63

Windrush. The famous beak-head doorway of St Peter's Church

stile, cut from one piece of stone, leading on through the fields to Great Rissington. A pair of King Charles spaniels eyed me from one of the wide window seats in the mill-house, looking exactly like their Staffordshire china counterparts. These models used to be called Keepers and were to be found on many a cottage mantelpiece. They were supposed to protect the family at night, when the husband was out poaching with his own dogs.

Beside the green in Windrush village is a disused cast-iron pumphead with a handsome lion front; once the main water supply, now a piece of Victoriana standing beside an age-old mounting block. Behind the wall are the baroque table tombs, with their roll tops and concave, shell-like ends surrounding ram's head carvings. The famous doorway into the church has a double row of carved beak-heads, almost as the stonemason left them in the twelfth century. The interior of the church is unusual, in that the chancel arch has 'barley-sugar' stone columns which lean sharply outwards to support the pointed arch. The columns which support the three-bay aisle arcade are short and thick, with sturdy moulded capitals and bases, a strong contrast to the delicate chancel columns. Outside the church, the village is mainly grouped around the green, the Manor, farms and cottages ranging in date from Tudor times to 1911, but sixty years is long enough for the local stone to weather and match its older neighbours.

A track from the Great Barrington road also leads down to Windrush Mill, built as a corn-mill in the seventeenth century. Windrush Camp, an Iron Age fort, is sited in the meadow beyond, barely distinguishable after centuries of ploughing. The Windrush river rarely rushes; it winds its long way slowly and gently through beautiful valleys. Rising above Temple Guiting, it passes through Naunton, Bourton on the Water, then, joined by the River Dikler and Sherborne Brook, it flows on to Burford, leaving the Cotswold country to join the Thames at Newbridge.

Beyond the village of Windrush, the river divides and forms a small island on which stands the Fox Inn; an inept name for an inn between trout and otter waters, which was the meeting place for the otter hounds.

Little Barrington is unique among the valley villages. It is set round a triangular green through which flows a brook. Well patronized by the village geese, the brook gushes out of a rock and finally disappears into a culvert. On the north-west side, the ground rises to form a crescent on which stands a group of cottages, including a terrace block and a converted smithy. So much quarrying went on in the surrounding district, it is a possibility that the crescent was the remains of an old quarry. Much of the stone came from mines which ran from the green, under the hill to the main A40 road. The old New Inn, now re-named The Inn for all Seasons, was built for the quarrymen and its cellars are reputed to be on the level of one of the mine passages. The early master masons were members of the Leper family, later followed by the Strongs. Timothy Strong had a quarry at Lower Barrington in 1617, probably situated in a field known as Humpty Dumpty Land. His son Valentine extended the mine passages in 1658 to supply stone for Queen's College, Oxford. There are traces of sluice gates on the Windrush, probably built to raise the level of the water and thus to allow stone to be loaded into barges.

St Peter's Church stands on another slight hill facing the cottage crescent. Originally Norman, it has fourteenth-century and fifteenth-century additions, traces of wall paintings and fragments of fourteenth-century glass. The Greenaway family memorials are in the chancel. Giles Greenaway built Barrington Grove in 1779 and planted the surrounding woodland.

Driving down the hill from the A40 in the early spring, the willows (*Salix chermissium*) behind the Fox Inn are brilliant orange, a breath-taking sight against the sombre evergreens in Great Barrington Park. St Mary's Church at Great Barrington is approached through the park; it is a Norman building completely restored in 1815. There are some amusing and beautiful monuments—one of the Bray children (1720) sensibly dressed in their outdoor clothes, being conducted over the clouds to Heaven by a winged angel. In the corner by the organ is the effigy of Captain Edmund Bray, his face and armour worn away by the constant sharpening of scythes and sickles, just the right stone for the job when the vicar was not about. Since the advent of the mowing machine, what is left of Captain Bray has been allowed to rest in peace.

Coming from a family of keen fishermen, I quote the fisherman's prayer to be found in the church, to the memory of Charles John Ryhis Wingfield:

> God grant that I may fish
> Until my dying day.
> And when it comes to my last cast,
> I humbly pray,
> When in my Lord's safe landing net
> I'm peacefully asleep,
> That in his mercy,
> I be judged good enough to keep.

The long stone bench with elbow ends, rejected by the restorers and now built into the churchyard wall, is a good evening bird-watching site. Thousands of starlings have roosts in many of the Cotswold woods and judging by the black clouds of them which came homing in, the high trees in Great Barrington Park are a popular centre. One cloud flew at speed, straight across the path of a small flock of black rooks, making their way home in a more leisurely fashion—to my surprise, the rooks quickly turned and flew back the way they had come.

Great Barrington village consists of a double row of houses along the street, mostly modernized in the 1950s but unspoilt. The original river bridge was built by Thomas Strong in the seventeenth century for the crossing of his heavily laden wagons of stone.

Nearby Wyck Rissington was the home of Gustav Holst, who as a young man was the organist at the church and lived in the village. The church guide recommends a walk through the maze in the rectory garden, pointing out that "Our life is a journey . . . the wrong turnings are the sins we make." A good many sinners emerge from that maze.

The Red Arrows were until recently stationed at Rissington Aerodrome. They had a pelican mascot billeted out at Birdland, where it consumed 7 pounds of fish a day. All sizes, shapes and nationalities of fish were welcomed into its enormous shopping-bag beak. The airfield is now to become a camp for the Royal Irish Rangers and the Red Arrows are attached to the R.A.F. Maintenance unit at Kemble Aerodrome.

High up on the wolds, there is a farmer who welcomes visitors from May to September. Most Cotswold farmers, alas with some cause, resent the influx of tourists and townees who without permission like to walk and picnic in their fields, but at Cotswold Farm Park they are welcome. Five miles out of Stow-on-the-Wold, on the B4077 road to Tewkesbury, is a turn to Bourton on the Water, and along this road, clearly marked, is the entrance and car park for visitors. There are no wild animals, it is an ordinary farm, raising wheat and barley for income, but the farmer, Joe Henson, has a hobby. Aided by the Rare Breeds Survival Trust, he has allocated 25 acres on which the public may see the many survivors of rare sheep and cattle which he is breeding. The 25 acres of uneven pasture land, quarried for tile-stones a century ago, is now laid out so that interested members of the public can walk around the paddocks, in which the rare, historic breeds are enclosed.

So many of the beautiful buildings in the Cotswolds were built by the rich wool merchants and their families, it is interesting to see the breeds of sheep which provided their wealth. Early in the twelfth century, Edward I had appreciated the value of English wool for export and to facilitate this trade founded The Merchants of the Staple, with licensed staple towns where wool could be bought and sold. His grandson, Edward III, married the Flemish princess Philippa of Hainault, who brought, as part of her dowry, the heavily fleeced Flemish sheep. These were crossed with the hardy Cotswold sheep, re-sulting in the famous 'Cotswold Lions'.

At Cotswold Farm Park, you can see the 'Lions', recognizable by their wide heads; their forelocks, true to tradition, are left unsheared. There are many other varieties, the Soays, small brown sheep, last survivors of the prehistoric domestic sheep of Europe; Orkney sheep, mainly seaweed feeders from North Ronaldsay; black, multihorned sheep from St Kilda; and Jacob's sheep, from which his son's 'coat of many colours' was possibly made. There are Manx Loghtans and Norfolk Horns, to name but a few.

Also there are all kinds of cattle—the Longhorns, nearest direct descendants of the wild cattle domesticated by Stone Age man; the Wild White Park cattle, brought here by the Romans for their 'bull cult' religious worship; Old Gloucesters, docile and popular, used as ploughing oxen in the Middle Ages. The milk from the cows of this breed is ideal for cheese making.

There are rare breeds of pigs, horses, donkeys, goats and poultry, the latter including the wild bush-turkeys brought here from America in Victorian times. Turkeys were not always our main Christmas fare. At one time it was swans and peacocks. Apart from the animal interest, the paddocks are on one of the highest of the wolds and the views from all the walks are superb; some sheltered seats are thoughtfully provided. I was up there one November,

Temple Guiting

the sunshine brilliant but the cold bitter, and I went into the warmth of the farm buildings to see a litter of piglets, bright tan with dark brown stripes, the progeny of a wild boar and a Tamworth sow. I saw young Longhorn bulls in the warmth of their pen, though bulls are not my favourite animal, since on one Cotswold walk I took a short cut across the fields, turned a corner round a hedge, and came face to face with the farmer's pedigree Hereford bull. I do not know which of us was the more surprised, but he reacted first. As I turned to rush back to a gap in the hedge,

his great warm nose tossed me over like a ball and I landed in the soft mud of the brook. Fortunately this was observed by the village bus driver, who waited for me with the greeting, "Playful, ain't 'ee? Best stand by my engine and dry off."

By the warmth of Mr Henson's log fire, grudgingly shared with us by two retrievers, I heard about the work of the Trust of which he is the chairman and of their ability to export pedigree stock to assist breeders all over the world. Since the Farm Park was first started, it has expanded to include a lecture hall, mainly used by schools, and a full-time education officer has joined the staff. The recently laid out farm trail is extremely popular and tired visitors may refresh themselves at the new café. An explanatory plan and leaflet on the farm trail gives information about stone walling, wild flowers, water supplies, crops—ranging from the bright yellow oil-seed rape to barley and wheat, and including deciduous woods and even stone gateposts.

Business over, we talked theatre, about his famous father Leslie Henson. "I leave acting to my young brother Nicky," he said. "Animals have always been my love, but I'm a born showman. If I have a rare breed, I like the public to enjoy it with me."

In spite of the November cold, it was a glorious day to explore the banks of the Windrush in the steep-sided valley down the lane from the farmhouse. It is possible to walk beside the river between the two Guitings, passing an old stone clapper bridge. Crossing the Windrush by the ford, the lane leads up the steep bank into Kineton and on to Temple Guiting. This is an old place; it was given to the Preceptory of Quenington, owned by the Order of Knights Templars, about 1150, at which time they worked a fulling mill at Barton. The church of St Mary has undergone many restorations and it has a 'Red Riding Hood' mode of entry—"Pull the string to lift the latch". The craftwork of the iron floor-grills, laced strip-iron in an intricate design, is extremely good. A sparrow chirruped at me from the lectern, cheekily perched on the handsome brass eagle.

Manor Farm, early sixteenth century, is said to have been the summer residence of the bishops of Oxford. It has a wall dovecote and is considered one of the finest small Tudor houses. Guiting House is more pretentious, with its garden front of three bays and Venetian window, but it is beautifully sited beside the Windrush and faces across the valley to the woods beyond. As most botanists know, Guiting Wood used to be a wild-flower Mecca, with more rare specimens to the square mile than anywhere else in the Cotswolds.

The large village green at Guiting Power, triangular in shape, slopes up the hill, as do the houses surrounding it. The village is a tidy little place and many of the houses have been well restored. The bakery on the corner of Well Lane emitted a delicious smell, but no amount of knocking produced the baker (who provides home-made bread and pies for the surrounding villages) until I discovered a bell on a side door.

Guiting Power

Guiting Power is one of the more fortunate Cotswold villages. The Lord of the Manor, Mr Raymond Cochrane, has set up the Guiting Manor Trust, to protect the village from the invasion of weekend second-home buyers. He has given most of his own 1,000-acre estate to finance the trust, which now owns many of the 109 houses in the village. These are rented to young people brought up in the country and wishing to remain there after marriage. An added attraction at Guiting Power for true country lovers is the No. 4 Nature Trail of the Gloucestershire Trust for Nature Conservation. Opened in 1965, it is approached from the footpath by the church and offers a variety of interests. There is a profusion of wild flowers, including water plants, it is a haunt of herons, kingfishers and badgers, and for those who like them, it is also a happy breeding ground for grass snakes.

From the Guitings, the Windrush winds along into Naunton, where the monastic landlords of Llanthony Abbey and St Oswald's Priory once vied with one another over the sheep rearing. If the river ran beside the village street, this place might be as popular as Bourton-on-the-Water, but the valley is much narrower and the river flows behind the houses. From any of the lane bridges, one can look along the river and see that a variety of small private bridges connect the houses and the gardens on either bank. The green is at the west end of the long street, with a good seat from which to admire the old houses grouped around it and the bridge over the Windrush. The sheltered gardens still boasted some late-flowering chrysanthemums, as bright a yellow as the winter jasmine.

In the church of St Andrew, the fourteenth-century pulpit, delicately carved in stone with canopied panels and pinnacled buttresses, is the greatest treasure, though almost rivalled by the rows of hassocks covered in petit-point work in beautiful designs, making a riot of colour as they hang in rows along the backs of the pews.

Naunton Manor was acquired in 1287 by Little Malvern Priory and held until the Dissolution. In the fields around Naunton, arrowheads of the Bronze and Neolithic periods have been found, also British and Roman coins. A find of interest to gardeners was the fossilized print of a leaf, possibly 250 million years old and since identified as that of a ginkgo tree. These trees are natives of China and specimens may be seen at the Arboretum at Moreton-in-Marsh.

Naunton suffered severely from the Great Plague of 1350 but the population increased in the nineteenth century, when the quarries were busy supplying tile-stones for the college roofs at Oxford. Quarrying is still a local industry.

Cromwell House, built about 1600, belonged to the

Naunton. The village stretches for a mile along the banks of the River Windrush, with many houses dating from 1600

Aylworth family. A John Aylworth, who built the Lady Chapel, was squire in the sixteenth century and it was Richard Aylworth who fought with the parliamentary forces which defeated the King's army at the battle near Stow-on-the-Wold in 1644. A rector of the church, Edward Arthur Litton, was a friend of Lewis Carroll, and Nauntonians like to boast that some of *Alice in Wonderland* was written in the rectory garden.

One of several horseshoe gates to be seen in the Cotswolds

CHAPTER FOUR

Stow to Stowell Park

The hamlet originally called St Edward Stow was on the Maugersbury manor estate belonging to the Abbey of Evesham. The abbots, keen businessmen, foresaw the need for a market in which to sell their flocks and fleeces. They received a royal grant for a market in 1107 and chose for their site the flat land on the hilltop, already crossed by the Roman Fosse Way. Unable to build beside the Fosse because it was a parish boundary, they made two diversionary roads to lead into their new, carefully laid out market centre of Stow-on-the-Wold. Some 800 feet above sea level, it is the highest town in the Cotswolds and in the centuries following its original conception, it steadily developed. The many roads now leading to it used to be thronged with drovers driving cattle and sheep from places as far distant as Wales, to what were the busiest markets in the Cotswolds. Modern travellers following the Fosse Way (A429) may be deceived into thinking that the town consists of no more than a row of pleasant stone houses between two petrol stations. The large market square lies behind these houses, here in the heyday of the wool trade as many as 20,000 sheep would have been penned for sale on market days. The village expanded and its many inns housed visitors who came to its thriving markets.

Stow suffered severely during the Civil War, when a battle was fought on the Donnington side of the village. Some 1,500 royalist prisoners were incarcerated in St Edward's Church, which was left in a ruinous condition. Stow remains a market town but only two fairs are held, in May and October, under charters granted by Edward IV in 1476. Nowadays, these are mainly pleasure fairs or mops; the important horse sales, under the control of a local auctioneer, are held in May and July. Walking along the lane from Maugersbury, I passed some gypsies camped on the verges, their horses being groomed for the May sale on the following day. Gypsies know all the tricks for making a horse appear lively. Their breakfast oats might be well sprinkled with powdered ginger and their drinking water laced with rum.

An incongruous mixture of ancient and modern appears on Stow's village green, where a neat row of plastic litter bins stands beside the old stocks, whose occupants used to have much of the town's rubbish thrown at them. St

73

Edward's House, now a café, has an elegant façade, with early eighteenth-century fluted Corinthian pilasters similar to those at Bedfont House in Chipping Campden. The stone slab seats on either side of the doorway are a heavy burden, judging by the haggard faces of the small stone lions which support them. Off the wide square the streets are extremely narrow. On a bend in Church Street is the St Edward's Grammar School, built in 1594 and now used as a Masonic Hall. Beside this is the path leading to the church of St Edward, built on a plot of land given by King Ethelred in 987. It was restored in the 1680s after the Civil War and again in 1847. Here is a large painting of the Crucifixion, attributed to Gaspar de Craeyer of Antwerp, a friend of Van Dyck and of Rubens, who regarded him as an extremely fine painter. It was brought from the Continent by the Chamberlaynes and presented to the church. There are memorials to the Chamberlayne family, who became lords of the Manor of Maugersbury.

Keyte or Keyt is an old Cotswold name and an incised floor slab in St Edward's Church is to the memory of Captain Hasting Keyt, killed in the Battle of Stow, 1646. More elaborate memorials to the Keyt family are in the Norman church at Ebrington, where the family held a manor in the parish for three centuries. Sir John Keyt, who is buried there with his wife, was a supporter of Charles I and raised a force to fight for the King, led by his son Hasting.

There is also a fine gilded tomb to Sir William Keyt, who in his will arranged a gift of "the milk of ten good and sufficient milch kine to the poor of Ebrington, from May 10th to November 1st annually, for ever". On his tomb is the Keyt coat of arms, a rebus kite above three trout. My friend Major Keyte, true to his arms, was a keen fisherman and bird watcher. While watching him cast a fly, I saw my first dipper, which flew out of the water like a leaping fish, skilfully dodging his baited hook.

I found a maker of corn dollies at Stow, hidden, rather like a dormouse, behind sheaves of straw, in a small, sixteenth-century cottage. Each variety of straw had a special quality and a special name—Maris Widgeon, White Emmer and Black Emmer. Maris Widgeon has long hollow stems, which can be joined by slipping one inside another. White Emmer is the straw of a Bronze Age type of wheat, specially grown for her by a local farmer. It has long whiskers, rather like barley, and these add an extra dimension to some of the traditional designs. It may be seen growing at the Avoncroft Building Museum, near Bromsgrove. The type I found most interesting was Black Emmer, which will not ripen in this country and has to be imported. I have seen fields of it growing in Turkey, a fascinating picture to paint, as the long black whiskers undulate in the wind like a dark, angry sea.

*Stow-on-the-Wold. The cross has a medieval base and the gabled head-stone
shows the abbot of Evesham receiving the royal charter from Henry I*

White Emmer ceased to be grown in this country when the long whiskers defeated the combine harvesters. Some of the corn-dolly designs are centuries old but consist of a few basic formations, mainly plaiting with three to seven straws. The versatility of the tradition was exemplified in a small round container, over a hundred years old, which had been made to hold a ball of wool. Such articles were made by sweated child labour, when the industry flourished in Suffolk. The example was a fine piece of craftsmanship, the delicate seven-plaited straws twisted round and round, with a delightful over-stitched star pattern.

Corn-dolly making is thriving again. They are in demand in the souvenir shops and visitors can see them being made at many of the county shows. There is also a growing export market. This busy lady was sensibly clad in a local sheepskin over good Cotswold knitting and was wearing wooden clogs to insulate her feet against the cold which rises from a stone-flagged floor.

Lower down the street, beyond the hexagonal Toll House, is the castellate 'Folly' of a Mr Enoch, who built it in 1848 to house his unofficial museum. It is now a private house, with a modern extension which might not have pleased the romantic Mr Enoch.

To the west of Stow, the road past the weir at Upper Swell leads to the old-established Donnington Brewery. Although this is private property, the lane runs alongside, and being high above, gives a good view down to the charming group of brewery buildings, the wall dovecote, the mill wheel, wildfowl reserve and the trout farm. The River Dikler rises on the brewery estate but has been dammed to form a large lake before rushing down to drive the mill wheel. It emerges from the mill race as a sizeable stream. The present owner of the brewery, Mr L. E. Arkell, explained to me the mysteries of good brewing and then we walked round his lake to see his private collection of wildfowl. A pair of tame black swans joined us, pecking at him for their titbits. Quite a number of regular visitors can be seen at various seasons on his lake, his peacocks squawking at them as they strut on the banks above.

Along the lane to Lower Swell are tracks which lead up to the long barrow and to a round barrow known as The Tump. The Hoar Stone and the Whittlestone, believed to have come from the long barrow, are preserved in the vicarage paddock. An Elizabethan legend tells how the Whittlestone was bewitched. When the wind was right and the clock on Stow church could be heard striking, the stone went to the well to drink. The old ladies of Swell, who dreaded to hear the clock strike, stayed indoors for fear of meeting the stone. The small church farther along the lane was largely restored in 1683 by Sir Robert Atkins, the Gloucestershire historian, when he acquired the

Donnington Brewery, a corn mill in the fourteenth century, later used by cloth weavers. Donnington's Ales have been on sale since 1865

Manor of Lower Swell, but much of the original Norman building remains.

The tympanum shows the skill of the Norman masons, being cut from ten stones so accurately as to look like one. The carved pagan symbol of the tree of life, with a dove pecking at a spray, is quite different work, as though the carver had been compelled to leave it half finished. The archway inside is twelfth century and leads to the old chancel. The present chancel is nineteenth century and has windows by Clayton and Bell, who were responsible also for the rather Pompeian murals of The Passion.

The more recent bellcote is in memory of the Rev. David Royce, another distinguished Gloucestershire historian, the vicar of this small church for fifty-two years. Before the Stow Museum was moved from St Edward's Hall to Bristol, it contained the Royce collection of prehistoric flints, arrowheads, and fragments of Roman tiles, pottery and ornaments, found in and around the Swells. Leaving the church door open to give more light, I was followed in by an inquisitive robin. He followed me round the church like a detective in a supermarket and flew into the church-yard only after seeing a gift left in the heavily padlocked collection box.

There was a time when woods covered the country between the Swells and Stow, for the country folk maintained that

> The squirrel can hop from Swell to Stow,
> Without resting his foot or wetting his toe.

It would have to be a jet-propelled flying squirrel to make that tree-top journey in the well-ordered agricultural lands which surround them today.

Living at the smithy in Lower Swell is a retired engineering instructor who had taught in many countries until his philosophy, his desire for a simple, carefree and unhurried life, brought him to Lower Swell. Working equally well in brass, copper, steel or wrought iron, his chief delight is to copy old gear mechanisms. Over the original fireplace in the smithy, he has set up a wind-dial, a replica of the one in Kensington Palace. The dial has a painted border, surrounding a Saxton's pictorial map of England. On the border, the four main and the four intermediate points of the compass are marked and as the pointer moves round, the smith can look up from his work and see which way the wind is blowing.

The Greek astronomer Andronicus built the 'Tower of the Winds' at Athens in 100 B.C., and his brazen Triton at the summit was turned round by the wind—the origin of the English weathervane. One Cotswold vicar, keener on sailing than on sermonizing, had a wind-dial fixed in his church, operated by the weathervane. When he noted a favourable wind, the sermon was cut short and his curate was left to bid goodbye to his flock while the vicar ran for his boat by way of the vestry door.

Having taught engineering in some of the Arab countries, Mr Nichols is interested in water clocks. I was shown a simple type which is still used in the agricultural fields of the East for timing the supply of water for irrigation. It consists of a large copper bowl of water, on which floats a smaller bowl which has a hole pierced in the base. The size of the hole determines the time it takes to sink.

Propped against the window was a different design of water clock, his copy of a Greek Clepsydra, one of the earliest time-measuring devices not dependent on shadows cast by the sun. The principle of this was the escape of water at a regulated pace through a small hole in the bottom of a water box. This was introduced into Britain by the Romans, who used them for timing the night watches of their armies. They were still in use in this country up to the eighteenth century, by those who could not afford mechanical clocks. In the smithy showroom were samples of well-designed fire baskets, lanterns and candlesticks.

The buildings in the village are of stone, one of the oldest being the seventeenth-century Golden Ball Inn, where the good Donnington Ale from the brewery at the source of the Dikler is in demand. Parties of the village boys, encouraged by the smith, try to keep the village tidy and the river free from weeds and rubbish, an example to be followed by any village lucky enough to have a river. Many of the houses around the Swells were restored by the architect Sir Edwin Lutyens, who designed the war memorial on the village green. His major work in the Cotswolds was the rebuilding of Abbotswood, on the hill which lies between Upper and Lower Swell. Bowl Farm on the Abbotswood estate was the site of Sir Robert Atkins's manor. The house was rebuilt in the early nineteenth century but the stable block is thought to be the original.

Although Lutyens designed New Delhi, he was not responsible for the extraordinary Hindu-style façade of a cottage on the road to Stow. This has pointed dormers crowned with fir-cones, a hooded doorway with pineapple decorations and elaborate ogee arched windows. The reason for this was to attract the public but the explanatory lettering on the wall plaque is now illegible and the passerby is left wondering what this strange little building is doing in a Cotswold lane. A mineral spring was discovered here in 1807 and it was hoped the place could be developed into a spa, hence the name Spa Cottage.

A walk from Lower Swell up to Chalk Hill brings one to the field path which leads over Eyford Hill where there are three round barrows and down past Eyford Park,

Upper Slaughter. The delightful buildings show the influence not only of the Normans but also of the sixteenth-century masons and of Sir Edwin Lutyens in 1906

Lower Slaughter with its cottages built along the banks of Slaughter Brook, a broad, shallow stream crossed by simple stone bridges

following the small River Eye as it flows into Upper Slaughter. The strange name of this charming village derives from *slohtre*, meaning a pool or muddy place. St Peter's Church, originally Norman, has suffered many restorations but contains a brass to John Slaughter (1583) and two later ones. Eight cottages facing on to the open square were remodelled by Sir Edwin Lutyens in 1906 and all the houses in the village are of stone from local quarries; most have stone roofs. Slaughter slates were available in 1452 and were used for New College, Oxford. The two manor houses offer visitors opportunities to see the interiors of these beautiful old buildings. The Manor House was built by the Slaughter family in the sixteenth century. They were mentioned in the reign of Henry II as the "de Sclotres". This family dispersed to America in the eighteenth century and many of the descendants and others are now able to avail themselves of the self-catering accommodation at this ancestral home.

The hotel named The Lords of the Manor was originally the parsonage. It was enlarged by the Witts family, (the lords of the manor), who made it their permanent home about 1855. Pleasant walks lead to the round barrows at Wagborough Bush, to Salters Pool, and on to Lower Slaughter. Out of season, there are no coach loads of visitors, no paddlers jumping off the low stone bridges, no weary tourists cooling their feet in the clear water of Slaughter Brook. Even crowded with people, it is an extremely beautiful village, with tall trees, and a mill with water wheel beside the brook, which makes a large curve as it winds between the stone buildings. The manor house in the centre of the village was built by Valentine Strong of Barrington, about 1640, for the Whitmore family who lived there until 1964. The sixteenth-century dovecote, one of the finest in Gloucestershire, can be seen from the road between the handsome stone gate piers of the drive. On the north bank of the brook, the older cottages are grouped round the green opposite the church. Even the council houses in this unspoilt village are roofed with traditional stone slates.

Lanes and a short section of the B4068 will take you from the Slaughters to a totally different type of landscape surrounding the village of Aston Blank or Cold Aston; the residents prefer the old name. Either way, it can be windswept, cold and bleak up there and at other times gloriously open and hot. The landscape was changed by the enclosures, which between 1715 and 1752 reduced the flocks feeding on common land from thousands to hundreds. The commissioners made new roads, cut across the commons as straight as the old Roman roads. This necessitated miles of stone walling, giving the countryside its present character. Fortunately the stone was readily available in the district at that time and walling labour was cheap, averaging 1s. 6d. a perch for walls 4 feet high.

In December the garden walls were covered with cotoneaster berries and yellow jasmine. Sounds of carol singing came from the village school and a poster announcing their Nativity Play was pinned to the massive trunk of the churchyard yew. The villagers say this is older than the church; it certainly has a girth of 16 feet, but much of St Andrew's Church is Norman. Yew trees have been known to live for over a thousand years, so at a possible 900 years old the villagers could be right. The village is mainly grouped round the green with its large sycamore tree, and the seventeenth-century Plough Inn also serves as the post office. It is a village of horses rather than cars, as it is a popular stud area. A string of hunters or golden Palominos, with their white manes and tails, or Welsh mountain ponies, are often to be seen passing by the village green.

Notgrove village is far less bleak, though some snow-break chestnut fencing protects the roads from drifts, near the lonely burial ground of Notgrove barrow. Since World War II, the whole village has become part of one estate and the buildings have been well restored. The main part is grouped around the green but the church is up on the hill, behind two farms. Parishioners may take the short cut past Manor Farm, but for visitors there is the longer lane through the Glebe Farm. In the church of St Andrew are the effigies of three Tudor and Stuart members of Dick Whittington's family, described by David Verey in his *Buildings of Gloucestershire* as "crude country work".

Having read of an embroidery at which twenty people had laboured for eleven years, I was half expecting some poorly designed, painstaking village stitching. Nothing of the kind! It is magnificent; well lit by lamps, focused on the excellent design by Colin Shelton Anderson, the work

Notgrove

Hampnett. The church of St George. The interior of this should not be missed, whatever you think of Victorian paintings!

covers the entire wall behind the altar. The three main panels show the village, the church and the manor house as they stand in the countryside. The panels are bordered with hazel, from which Notgrove takes its name, and this is entwined with the emblems and crests of the twenty embroiderers. It is as arresting in this small church as the

Sutherland tapestry at Coventry Cathedral, and this is not a loom-made tapestry; it has been patiently stitched in gros and petit point. I envied the carved angels who could look down on it every day.

The lane from Notgrove to Northleach passes through the Saxon settlements of Turkdean and Hampnett. For walkers there are the remains of one of the Enclosure Commissioners' roads, a white stony track past Grove Farm down to Breakwater Bottom beside the main road. The lane passes through Turkdean, where the terrain changes again. Gay Ward's poem 'Trees' describes the steep bank of beautiful beech trees—"Flickering, shivering, endlessly quivering" which divides the village into two parts, Upper and Lower. Turkdean Manor (1588) and the sixteenth-century Rectory and Manor Farm are all interesting buildings, and on the high ground the church of All Saints has many surviving Norman features, also a surprising screen, added in 1949 and painted in vivid colours. Below the bank of beeches is Lower Dean House and the small village which was part of the separate manor held by Llanthony Priory.

The lane dips and rises again, crossing an excellent walk from Puesdown Inn to Farmington past the remains of an ancient cross before reaching the small group of buildings and the large barn by Hampnett's church of St George. This is a small Norman church with the whole of the chancel painted in a stencilled pattern of unbelievable garishness, the work of a Victorian rector, the Rev. W. Wiggins, who must have been taught how to use a stencil but did not know when to stop; the Cotswolds are full of surprises!

Beyond Prison Copse and at the junction of the Fosse Way and the A40 stands the façade of a 'House of Correction'.

Sir George Paul for Prison-house renowned,
A wandering knight on high adventure bound.
(Anon.)

The prison was designed in 1789 by William Blackburn for Sir George Onesiphorus Paul. The Pauls were Huguenot immigrants who established themselves in Gloucestershire in the seventeenth century. They were great believers in biblical names and Onesiphorus, a surname from the Book of Timothy, did not manage to adopt the more popular name of George until 1780. Sir George was a strange character, whose early life followed the usual pattern of rich young society blades. He made the Grand Tour in 1767, was a member of Boodle's Club and of the Dilettanti Society—then suddenly he tired of it all and spent the rest of his life studying and improving the English penal system. In 1783, England's prisons were in dire need of reform. Criminals of all ages and both sexes were herded together in one large room, with no occupation and no exercise available. They were lucky if they were moved into another room at night and this rarely had any bedding straw. Many died of a form of typhus called gaol fever, possibly carried by body lice, which multiplied in the filthy prison conditions. Lice were always on the move searching for a host and they left a dead body as soon as it was cold, as Gordon Bottomley describes in 'King Lear's Wife':

A louse crept out of my lady's shift,
A-hum, A-hum, A-hee.
Crying Oi Oi we are turned adrift.
The lady's bosom is cold and stiff
And her armpit's cold for me.

There was a kind of rough justice about this highly contagious disease. When prisoners were taken to court to receive their long and usually unjust sentences, the officials and the judges oft-times caught the disease. At the Black Assizes, held in Cambridge in 1522, all the judges died of gaol fever. The lice crept across the court to juicier victims.

Paul decided to change all this. He built five new prisons in Gloucestershire, including the one at Northleach.

85

In these, reforms were introduced—day and night rooms, exercise yards, baths, an infirmary and a chapel were provided. Nothing now remains of the Northleach prison but the grey façade at the crossroads, with its rough quoins and two side pavilions. It is dismissed by many passing motorists as someone's folly.

The village of Northleach has suffered many ups and downs and in spite of its long history it is not at first sight an attractive place, the heavy traffic which rushes along its main street makes it difficult to appreciate the old buildings. But in the fifteenth century, it was an important centre of the wool trade, which the 'Cely Papers', a series of letters written between 1475 and 1488, describe so well. The Celys were wool merchants in Mark Lane, London, who bought most of their wool from the Midwinters of Northleach, before exporting it to the European markets. Judging by the tombstones in the churchyard, the descendants of the Midwinters continued to live in and around Northleach for a further 400 years and thus witnessed many of the town's misfortunes. A company of Fairfax's soldiers came to the town after the Battle of Naseby and raided the handsome church, fortunately leaving undamaged two of the original figures over the porch entrance. The Midwinters saw the decline in the wool trade, when the spinners and weavers had to move further south to the mills near Stroud. The weak flow of the water of the River Leach proved insufficient to provide enough power to drive the mill wheels.

The decline in the wool trade caused great distress in the seventeenth century and successive governments tried to revive it. A law was passed which ordered that a corpse must be wrapped in wool before burial. In 1678, a fine of £5 was imposed to try to stop the persistent evasion. The act was ignored, though not repealed until 1800. Alexander Pope was inspired to write the following—

> Odious woollen! T'would a saint provoke . . .
> No, let a charming Chintz or Brussels lace
> Wrap my cold limbs, and shade my lifeless face!

Business picked up in 1750, when the new road from London to Gloucester brought the coaches through Burford and Northleach, resulting in many inns in the main street. The Red Lion, with its overhanging half-timbered upper storey, conspicuous in a row of stone buildings, remains an inn. The King's Head has become Walton House, and the Antelope, which existed in 1570, is hidden behind the Victorian Institute.

The coming of the railways ended the coaching trade and money was scarce again, though some carriers made a small living at the stations. One carrier had to drive his old horse with loads far beyond its strength. When it fell dead

*Northleach. The market place, overlooked by the great wool church of St
Peter and St Paul*

in the shafts, the carter scratched his head and said: "That's strange, I've never know 'im do that afore."

The church, largely rebuilt in the fifteenth century by the rich wool merchants, stands behind what was the market square, nowadays cluttered with parked cars. On one side of the path to the churchyard gate is the six-teenth-century Old Wool House, disfigured by the instal-lation of large picture windows. Behind the Post Office and supermarket, its windows pasted with the usual '2p off' posters, is the lock-up, identified by a crude card-board notice on the door. Once inside the churchyard, one is in a different world. On the left is an ancient barn, with a rare columbarium, an arrangement of four stag-gered rows of pigeon holes, which run the whole length of the building except for the portion over the great oak beam which spans the high cartway—here, there is barely space for one row.

The church itself is one of the great wool churches of the Cotswolds. Both exterior and interior are extremely beautiful and it was recently restored by Sir Basil Spence and reseated with chairs made in the Gordon Russell workshops in Broadway. On a pre-Christmas visit, many of the chairs were occupied by a wriggling group of eager children. They were being called out in turn to audition for their Nativity Play. The schoolmaster was standing well up the aisle, calling sternly "Speak up! Speak up! I can't hear you!" A small girl standing in front of the altar steps and obviously in some confusion about the part of Mary was shouting despairingly "But I'm not married! I'm not married!"

The church contains many fine brasses perpetuating the names of the town's wool merchants. These metal sheets originally came from the Low Countries and were exported from Cologne, hence their old name 'Cullen plates', though they were cut and engraved in England. The oldest brass in St Peter's, dated 1400, is in memory of a wool merchant and his wife, but is so mutilated that the name cannot be deciphered. The brass to William Mid-winter and his wife, dated 1501, shows them appropriately resting with their feet on sheep; but the best examples of period brass engraving are those commemorating the Fortey family. That of John Fortey (1459) has wreathed medallions in the border, incorporating his initials and his trade mark; his feet rest on a woolsack. The brass to Thomas Fortey and his wife (1501) must have been an ex-tremely fine example when it was complete, and records that Thomas was a renovator of churches and also of roads, which in the Middle Ages was regarded as an act of piety. There is a large range of brasses in fair condition, which in my student days provided lucrative rubbings. It used to amuse us, as the faces of the wealthy old wool mer-chants began to appear on our paper, to think that they were still responsible for financial transactions so many years after their death.

The clerestory, which includes a nine-light window over the chancel arch, was added by John Fortey, who with his father Thomas may also have been responsible for the Lady Chapel, which bears the date 1489. Another beautiful item is the magnificent embroidered altar cloth, which covers the original ten foot long stone altar. The cloth was designed by Comper and embroidered by the Sisters of Bethany. Anyone who knows the practical difficulties of embroidering with gold and silver threads will appreciate the painstaking work. This glittering altar cloth is enhanced and well lit by the modern window designed by Christopher Webb in 1963.

The lane at the end of the churchyard crosses the small River Leach and a footpath leads to a track called Helen's Ditch, which takes you to the hamlets of Upper End and Eastington. The old name of the latter was Northleach Foreign when it was held by St Peter's Abbey, Gloucester. The manor appears to have been a fifteenth-century mill house with later additions. The circular dovecote has a conical roof and lantern which could also be fifteenth century. A pleasant walk along the lane brings you back to the Burford end of Northleach's long street, near the nineteenth-century hospital. Returning to the market square, you pass the Dutton almshouses, built in 1616 by Thomas Dutton, whose family owned the manor of Eastington after the Reformation.

On the south side of what is still called The Green are two narrow lanes of old houses. Tudor House, with a stone-built ground floor and jettied half-timbered first floor, was the home of John Fortey. His packhorses and wagons, heavily laden with Cotswold fleeces, must have passed between the stone corbels of the carriage entrance five centuries ago, their journey eased on the roads repaired by his pious but businesslike father, Thomas Fortey.

The through traffic makes it almost impossible to view Northleach with any enjoyment, though in 1961, an excellent bus shelter was built, using local material. The seats in this face the market square and enable one at least to appreciate the beauty of the church tower. The real beauty of the Northleach buildings, their weathered stone roofs and the church tower, may be seen from the steep lane which approaches the town from Farmington; up there, the busy A40 is entirely hidden.

Provided the weather is dry, the Cotswold countryside is full of interest in the winter and remarkably free of people. Just south of Northleach is the lane to the Roman villa at Chedworth. Along the top of the wolds here is a windbreak, the Puesdown Beeches, about thirty feet wide, tall trees, closely planted. This winds its way for miles, from Stowell Park down to Hampnett. In midwinter, even though the beeches were bare of leaves, they effectively blocked the magnificent view of the hills which drop down to Listercombe Bottom and rise again to the woods around Yanworth and Chedworth. The noise of the car along the lane between two fields of winter wheat put up a flock of crested plovers, which rose into the wind, swirling this way and that, first black, then white, like a flock of turnstones. The lane drops steeply into the valley and although driving slowly in low gear, it was difficult to avoid the pheasants. In the Cotswolds, their strutting and display is described as 'kyolloping' and they were certainly kyolloping, for their brilliant plumage was scintillating in the sunlight. Down in the valley, they were following a bull as he grazed, disturbing the frosty earth for them by the sheer weight of his enormous frame. Sooner them than me! I was glad of the drystone wall between us as he raised his broad head to give a misty bellow.

Pheasants have been bred (and poached) in the Upper Coln valley for centuries. Lord Stowell's gamekeeper was shot by a poacher in 1831 and James Joy from Withington was transported for seven years, at a time when the notorious 'Game Laws' were in effect. Little thought was given by the wealthy landowners to the poverty of their tenants, who could only appeal to the parish for help.

Along the ledge of the hill is a wonderful view of the woods, before the lane enters them and leads to the site of the villa. There, it stops and offers a variety of beautiful walks—to the long barrow in Withington Woods, to the site of the Roman temple in Chedworth Woods, and further up the hill, to another Roman site lying between Compton Abdale and Casey Compton. In mid-December, sheltered by a horseshoe of wooded hills rising steeply around the villa, it was possible to sit outside and enjoy the long views and the colour of the larches, which still retained the bright tan of their autumn foliage. The Romans chose beautiful positions with good water supplies for their villas.

The pheasants had been a delight on the ground, and above, there was a display by three Red Arrows in the sky.

"Worth watching!" said the curator at the villa. "They do their homework over here most days." Their brilliant colour was catching the sun like the plumage of the pheasants. Eighteen centuries had passed since the building of the Roman wall on which I sat to marvel at the great variety of baths at the Chedworth villa—hot, cold, sauna or Turkish. Did the Roman ladies have any time for housework or were they well staffed with slaves?

The water supply came from a spring which was covered by a small apsidal building, the Nymphaeum. Inside was an octagonal reservoir holding 1,500 gallons;

this continues to supply the present site. The original approach to the villa was from the White Way, which passed close to the barrow from which came the cremation urn now in the museum. The hunting relief came from a square pagan temple near the River Coln.

The site is National Trust property, beautifully laid out, with every room clearly labelled. The museum was built by Lord Eldon on the east side of the inner court in 1866. It contains many interesting exhibits and it is worth looking for the portable pocket-size altars. Some humorous Roman artist must have enjoyed himself engraving Mars and Minerva. If it had not been for one of Lord Eldon's rabbiting parties digging out their ferret, Chedworth Villa might still be unknown to us.

The village of Chedworth, with many good stone houses, straggles along the valley. The church of St Andrew is late Norman, the original parts of the Manor House medieval, and on the hill above the house was a preceptory of the Knights Templar from Quenington.

At Yanworth, the church is lower down the valley beyond the short village street and is hidden away behind Church Farm, within an interesting group of buildings. The great barns, some with outside steps, dwarf the small church which faces the stone farmhouse across a wide yard. It has Norman foundations and there are the remains of wall paintings. The tower must be the smallest in the

Chedworth village, seen from the Seven Tuns, with the fine Norman church of St Andrew on the rising ground. The early use of Arabic numerals on the turret, dated 1485, reminds us of the village's international wool trade

county for it rises but a few feet as a continuation of the wall of the nave. There are said to be seven scratch dials and the two on the west of the porch are easy to find, as is the bracket dial above the porch.

St Leonard's Church at Stowell is in the grounds of Stowell Park. Along a bend in the well-kept drive is a group

91

of farm buildings and cottages surrounding a tree-lined yard. The way to the church on the left is up a double flight of stone steps leading from this yard. It was lunchtime and the yard appeared to be deserted, but a head popped out of a parked van and through a munch of sandwich, a friendly voice called "The key's in the notice box—light's behind the door." My chief interest was the wall painting and what is left of an early Doom fresco of about 1150. The Heavenly Court and the Twelve Apostles are looking down on the souls below, where there appear to be more saved souls than lost ones.

Stowell Park was built about 1600 for Sir Robert Atkinson, Recorder of Oxford, and enlarged for the Earl of Eldon in 1886. He was the benefactor who encouraged the excavations of the Chedworth Villa, which was on the Stowell estate land. Unfortunately, Stowell Park, with a water mill complete with its machinery and fed by the River Coln, is not open to the public.

The water wheel at Donnington Brewery, still in good working order

92

CHAPTER FIVE

Compton Abdale to the Shiptons

Compton Abdale's stone crocodile

Higher up the valley above Chedworth Woods is the small village of Compton Abdale, once known for its stone crocodile. This strange beast is almost unrecognizable, worn smooth with age, covered with moss, and lying in a damp corner where the water gushes from its mouth to become the small stream which flows beside the road. Here is another change in the terrain, for the church of St Oswald is built on a cliff above the village street, with a handrail provided for the steep climb up to the church door. The distinguishing feature is the tower, a landmark for miles around. It was built when the church was a possession of St Oswald's Priory at Gloucester, and is crowned with grotesque gargoyles. Heraldic beasts with staves form the pinnacles—poor brothers of those on St George's Chapel at Windsor. In spite of the exposed position, hart's-tongue ferns grow in profusion between the stones at the base of the tower. The view from here of the buildings below demonstrates how unsuited blue slate roofs are to Cotswold stone buildings.

From Compton, the Salt Way leads high up on to the wolds. I digressed, and took the pleasant drive through Salperton Park, to see the Doom painting in All Saints' Church. The house has been turned into flats and the path to the church, hidden amongst the trees, is at the side and

93

Salter's Hill, the highest point on the old Salt Way, running up from Roel Gate. On a clear day there is a view over Winchcombe to the valley of the River Avon

approached across the front garden. The painting on the north wall of the tower arch is well preserved and Death is depicted as a skeleton, spear at the ready, a bony hand on the wheel of life to stop at his command. This speeded me on my way to the windy heights of the old sheep country at Roel Gate. From this lonely crossroads, the only sign of habitation is an occasional farmhouse sheltering from the winds in a fold of the hills. It is a sky world with only the breezes and the birds for company. C. D. Lewis describes it so perfectly in his poem 'You that love England'.

> . . . The slow movement of clouds in benediction,
> Clear arias of light trailing over her uplands.

From these uplands, you can look down on miles and miles of open country rolling away into the blue distance. Flocks of yellowhammers, greenfinches and hedge sparrows flashed past in search of food. On the lane which leads down the hill to Roel Farm, three crows were lunching on the remains of a rabbit, their black feathers upright in the wind. There was once a village at Roel, one of the lost villages of England, where 200 people died of the Black Death. Their cottages and the church were allowed to fall into decay; country folk believed the dread disease lingered on in the stones. On the side wall of Roel Farm, there is a buttress and a trefoil-headed lancet window, which is believed to be all that remains of the church.

During the Civil War, Roel Farm was used as a refuge by Lord Chandos and the inhabitants of Sudeley Castle. The end wall shows signs of the church architecture, which can be clearly seen from the lane above the farm buildings and from the small stream which rushes past the farm to join the River Windrush. For walkers, there is a path from Hawling over the uplands, past Roel Hill Farm, to Deadmanbury Gate, at the corner of Guiting Wood. This meets the paths leading to Hailes and Stumps Cross.

After leaving Roel Gate, the Salt Way follows the high ridge above Spoonley Woods, in which are the remains of a Roman villa. Waterhatch lies in the bottom of the valley and one can see across the site of another villa at Wadfield, as the hills rise up towards Belas Knap. At the top of Sudeley Hill a thoughtful farmer has fenced off part of a field as a picnic area, where visitors can gaze on this magnificent country in peace; the lanes are too narrow for parking. The Salt Way keeps to the high ground, *en route* for Hailes Abbey, but the lane drops down through the beech woods, giving a splendid view of Sudeley Castle before climbing steeply to join the main street at Winchcombe.

Although there is little evidence remaining in the present town, I found it fascinating to walk the paths once trodden by the Saxons in what was their capital of Mercia.

95

The town has lacked the guiding hand of an F. L. Griggs; it rather reminds one of an old lady who has long since ceased to be particular about her appearance—a hotch-potch of shop fronts has been allowed to spoil the old buildings. The River Isbourne, which flows down the side of Castle Street to the tannery, may easily be mistaken for a ditch. The Abbey grounds are closed to the public, the church is hidden by a high stone wall, and only the brilliant golden weathercock high on the tower is indicative of the glories which lie beneath. Traffic fills the main street, mainly *en route* from Broadway to Cheltenham, though many tourists stop to enjoy the varied attractions offered at Sudeley Castle. Given the leisure to wander around and walk along the many footpaths radiating from the town, the antiquity and past history begin to take hold. Neolithic man made Belas Knap on the hill above the town by Humblebee Wood; the Romans built their villas in the folds of the hills; the Saxon King Kenulf founded the Abbey, which in 788 accommodated 300 monks, and this soon began to attract great wealth and learning to the settlement.

When Hailes Abbey was founded only a short distance away in the thirteenth century, the abbots of the two monasteries became the most powerful landowners and dominated the lives and education of the people until the Dissolution. Hailes had many relics which attracted pilgrims who came in their thousands. The wealthier pilgrims stayed at the Old George Inn at Winchcombe, where part of the pilgrims' gallery remains, thanks to the restoration ordered by Mrs Dent of Sudeley.

Richard Kyderminster was the abbot at Winchcombe from 1488 to 1525. Educated at Oxford, he was an astute man, an erudite teacher, and it was in his time that the abbey began to be regarded as a small university. The library was enlarged, the monks well taught and eager to pass on their knowledge. Revenues increased and the abbey flourished in every way. The original endowment of 13,000 acres had steadily increased to 25,000. The abbots must have been hard-hearted rent collectors, as old records show that if money was not available, almost anything was extracted from their tenants in lieu of rent. They forfeited their horses, harness, gloves and spurs—even flowers, for gillyflowers and roses are recorded as payments.

Still facing Queen's Square is the stout stone wall which Richard Kyderminster had built to enclose the abbey grounds. He did not live to see the utter destruction of his beloved abbey behind the wall. Due to ill health, he retired as abbot in 1525 and died in 1531. His successor, Abbot Richard Anselm, had to hand over the abbey to Sir John Brydges, who is reputed to have made an enormous personal profit as the result of the sale of the abbey treasures and the dressed stones resulting from the demolition

Winchcombe. The galleried yard of the George Inn. Carved in the spandrels of the doorway are the initials of Richard Kydderminster, who resigned as abbot in 1525

of the buildings. He was later made Lord Chandos, and in 1540 Thomas Cromwell, Vicar-General to Henry VIII, was duly informed: "We have despatched Haylys and Winchcombe."

The destruction of the abbey brought great poverty to the townspeople. Many had been employed by the monks, others had profited from the thousands of pilgrims, while the poor had received doles and had been regular recipients of monks' loaves. Stark poverty faced them. They turned to handicrafts of every kind, but it was difficult to market their goods, though glove-making survived as a cottage industry well into the nineteenth century.

To help the suffering town, Queen Elizabeth I granted a fair and a market, but following the rise in the cost of wheat in the seventeenth century, 4,000 beggars were recorded. This figure was only reduced to 2,000 by 1931. Having lived in the country between two workhouses, I suspect that many of this recorded 2,000 were the happy-go-lucky tramps who trekked daily from one workhouse to another, touching the gullible on the way.

Some Winchcombe folk grew the new, fashionable tobacco and in spite of the cost, difficulties and many processes involved in producing the final dried, rolled leaves, they managed to make a good profit. Tobacco Field, by the Cheltenham road, and Tobacco Close are reminders of these times. The tobacco growers were eventually taxed out of business by the Parliament of Charles II, whose policy was to aid the Virginian planters. The stout Winchcombites defied the prohibition order until finally soldiers were sent in to destroy their plants. James I had foreseen the evil effects of smoking and today's lung-cancer campaigners might well quote his words of 1604: ". . . loathsome to the eye, hateful to the nose, harmful to the braine, dangerous to the lungs . . . stinking fumes . . . resembling the horrible Stygian smoke of hell".

Most bird lovers know Winchcombe as the home of Christopher Merrett, who was born there in 1614 and whose family kept the Crown Inn which stood on the corner of Mill Lane. He became a doctor and was the first Librarian of the Royal College of Physicians. He is famous for his great work *Pinax*, which contains the first printed list of birds.

Folk walking along the path to the church of St Peter adjoining the site of the abbey are overlooked by a row of gargoyles. One wonders which of the friends or enemies of the old stonemasons are caricatured in this way—particularly the sour-faced man who is wearing a tall hat and is equipped with a pair of wings. The gargoyle with the large moustache and pointed, devil-like ears is said to be Ralph Boteler. When the present church was built in 1470 by Abbot William Winchcombe, Ralph Boteler gave much of his wealth towards its completion.

In the church are a few treasures rescued from the abbey ruins, a door with the initials R.K. and some tiles. It is possible that these tiles, like those in the museum at Hailes, were made by the travelling Malvern tilers. They found clay deposits at Greet, near the road to Broadway, which were later used by the pottery established there in 1800. The Cistercian Order was well known for its inlaid tiles, dating from the thirteenth century, and designed to record the coats of arms of its benefactors.

Mrs Emma Dent was responsible for the framing of the abbey tiles now displayed in the church. The Dent family bought Sudeley Castle in 1830, at which time it had degenerated into an alehouse—The Castle Arms. They restored some of the ruins and Winchcombe owes much to Mrs Emma Dent, a distinguished writer and historian. She was responsible for rescuing many local antiquities, and some were housed in the castle while others formed the nucleus of an excellent museum in the church tower, opened in 1928. The museum treasures were assembled by Miss Eleanor Adlard of Postlip. Since her death in 1967, the Adlard family has financed the removal of the museum to a larger room in the Town Hall.

To help fight vandalism, which is not a modern problem. Edward VI decreed that alms boxes should have three locks and could only be opened when the vicar and two churchwardens were present. The balustrade alms box at St Peter's with three locks is still in good condition.

The encased altar cloth, made from the cope of a fourteenth-century priest, was reassembled and the border added in the time of Catherine of Aragon. It is embroidered with her pomegranate badge and is thought to have been stitched by her while staying at Sudeley Castle.

Anne Boleyn, the second of Henry VIII's queens, also came to Sudeley to enjoy the hunting and the "salubrious air". The last of Henry's six wives, Queen Catherine Parr, came to live at Sudeley after his death, when she married her fourth husband, Baron Seymour of Sudeley. Her year at Sudeley in 1548 was gaily social, but she died in childbirth in 1549. Rumour has it that she was poisoned by her husband, Thomas Seymour, so that he could be free to court the young Queen Elizabeth, but, like so many over-ambitious Tudor schemers, he was beheaded on Tower Hill and his property passed to the Chandos family.

Few of the Winchcombe streets have name plates and Castle Street is not the road leading out of the square to the castle; this is nearer the centre of the town and follows the Isbourne to Tanyard Bank. In workshops near the tannery are two dedicated craftsmen, Keith Jameson and Bryant Fedden, who work in stone, metals and glass; many modern commercial firms have commissioned work from them. Examples of their craft can be seen in Gloucester Cathedral and Tewkesbury Abbey, and the topograph on

Hailes Abbey

Fish Hill near Broadway is also theirs. At the other end of the town, on the Broadway road, the Pottery at Greet, developed by Michael Cardew, is managed by another master potter and one-time partner of Cardew, Raymond Finch. Cardew, like his friend Gordon Russell, was a pioneer of good design. At the beginning of World War II he was given a government post to develop peasant pottery in West Africa. The work at Greet is mainly commercial oven-glaze ware, with a showroom displaying their more decorative work in the Cardew tradition. In two sheds at the bottom of the pottery garden, adjacent to Cardew's crumbling brick kiln, two young men are working in wood, one a wood turner with good original ideas, in great demand for all kinds of period restorations, while the other designs and makes excellent furniture; his sculpture in wood includes many interesting pieces.

In addition to the delightful walks in the grounds of Sudeley Castle (open to the public from March to October), there is a choice of good hill walks around Winchcombe. The ruins of Hailes Abbey, beautifully kept by the Department of the Environment, lie in a hollow of the hills and offer a walk full of history, especially in the museum and the nameless village church. The abbey was founded in 1246 by Richard, Earl of Cornwall, brother of Henry III and son of King John. Richard, who had already claimed extensive lands in Gloucestershire, was crowned King of the Romans when the German Empire was leaderless in 1257. He was able to endow the abbey liberally and the foundation was colonized by the Cistercian monks from Beaulieu, which had been founded by his father.

The church was built in 1130, before the Cistercian abbey, and contains thirteenth-century wall paintings which include the heraldic devices of the Earl of Cornwall and those of the castles of Eleanor of Castile, which appear again on the tiles. Some of these beautiful examples of the craft of the tilers employed by the Cistercians are thirteenth century and may have been rescued after the destruction of the abbey. A complete tiled floor taken from the abbey was built into the fifteenth-century mansion of Southam Delabere, near Cheltenham, built for the de la Beres whose memorials are in the church at Cleeve.

A field walk takes you to Didbrook, where the church was rebuilt in 1475 by William Whitchurch, Abbot of Hailes. It contains interesting period furnishings, pews, benches and a pulpit with a sounding board. All these are lit by reassembled fifteenth-century glass, enhanced by the beautiful windows of Edward Payne, added in 1961, which incorporate scenes of village life. Many of the stone cottages in the village are timber-framed, showing a fifteenth-century cruck construction rarely discernible in buildings of Cotswold stone.

On the other side of Winchcombe, the Cheltenham road climbs Cleeve Hill, where walks lead up to Cleeve Cloud, the highest land on the Cotswold escarpment. Many walks radiate from Cleeve Common to the valleys below, across to Belas Knap, to Chedworth, and to the woods above Postlip Hall. This sixteenth-century hall was for many years the home of the various owners of the Postlip paper mills. It is now leased to a group of young people, artists, sculptors and musicians, who, as so many have done before them, are trying to live as a commune. With the help of the Postlip Society, the fifteenth-century tithe barn, is used from time to time for concerts, poetry readings and exhibitions. It is furnished with church pews and a stage and has its own approach road. The small stone figure on the barn is reputed to be Sir William de Postlip, who lived at a previous hall in the reign of King Stephen. In those days, the lodge and the present drives did not exist. The old road went down the hill, past the pond and through the present mill property, to Winchcombe.

In the seventeenth century, the Durham family, then living at Postlip Hall, converted the abbey corn mill to the manufacture of paper. Various types of paper have been made there ever since and today, the filter papers made by Evans and Adlard are exported all over the world. Nothing is left of the old corn mill and the early machinery has been presented to the Paper Museum in London.

Mr Adlard gave me a book about the paper mills written by his aunt, Eleanor Adlard, and published as a memorial to her. It is printed on superb hand-made paper. It ends with the philosophical jingle which used to be sung in the rag-pickers' yards in Birmingham.

> Rags make Paper,
> Paper makes Money,
> Money makes Banks,
> Banks make Loans,
> Loans make Beggars,
> Beggars make Rags.

The abbey mill pond is fed by tributaries of the Isbourne and is used as a reservoir for the mill, but is well stocked with fish for the boys of Winchcombe.

On the hill above Postlip Hall is the mid twelfth-century chapel of St James, which was severely restored in 1890 for use as a Roman Catholic church. Later, services were held only once a year, and it is now closed. Below the Norman doorway, with its recessed tympanum ornamented with fish scales, the door has some unusual ironwork. The drop handle is backed by a sunburst and the escutcheon is within a beautifully worked plate six inches square. Near this old deserted chapel, standing alone at the edge of the wood, stood a bright scarlet metal construction by a member of the commune, an excellent piece of modern craftsmanship, which indicated the path back to the road.

The walk up to Belas Knap, on the hill above Humblebee How Plantation, even for those uninterested in ancient burial grounds, is well worth the climb. The enormous stones of the burial chamber show Neolithic man's knowledge and skill in stone work. The striking feature of this barrow, 170 feet long by 60 feet wide, is the false entrance at the north end, which is set back in a porch of drystone walling. Layer upon layer of thin stones were meticulously laid and strongly bonded. Although repaired in 1931, it is the oldest example of building in Cotswold stone, four to five thousand years old. The barrow was first excavated in 1863, when thirty human remains were found in the burial chambers. Against the false entrance were the bones of a man and of five children, thought to have been sacrificial burials of Beaker folk. The name Belas Knap is much later and means a beacon mound. This is open to the public at any time. Up there, the high wolds meet the sky; a place where the simple grandeur of nature fills one with awe.

The walk past West Wood drops downhill to the ancient hamlet of Charlton Abbots, a possession of Winchcombe Abbey. Between the woods and the stream, the monks founded their leper hospital near the spring which flows into a stone trough. The lazar house was given to the abbey by King Kenulf as a leper hospital. Lazar houses were so called after the French monastic order of St Lazarus. In 1313, the monks in France, defying the King's command, refused to carry out the medieval practice of burning all lepers. Instead, they set up institutions named Lazarettos for 'Christ's Poor', where the lepers lived and were cared for by the many monks who had also contracted the disease. Leprosy became prevalent in England after the return of the Crusaders. As a result of the policy of isolation and the strict but harsh treatment of the lepers practised by the hundreds of religious foundations which cared for them, England was free of the disease by the end of the sixteenth century.

Lepers were dragged from their families, who invariably tried to hide them, and the last rites were pronounced by the parish priest—"Henceforth be dead to the world and live with God." Living with God meant going round like ghosts, wearing long hooded robes, gloves, overshoes and masks. Lepers were compelled to speak in whispers and continually sound a bell or rattle, if outside the hospital precincts. They picked up food placed for them on the ground and any money they used for purchases had to be placed in jars of vinegar before it could be accepted by a trader. John Keble, in his poem about lepers, writes

103

Who would have thought our nature's strain
Was dyed so foul, so deep in grain?

Leprosy returned to this country when the immigration restrictions were lifted, but since 1957 cases are confined in one hospital.

The small church at Charlton Abbots is hidden behind the farm buildings of the Elizabethan manor house. There are no helpful signposts, but it is rewarding to find the stone path beside the barns, for at the end is the view of the valley of the Isbourne and of the hills beyond. The church, due to dilapidation, was restored at the end of the nineteenth century, but the present bell came from the old church and must have been heard by hundreds of lepers, as it is said to have been cast by John of Gloucester around 1346.

For those unable to make the climb to Cleeve Cloud and enjoy the walks, the low road is sheltered and mysterious as it winds its way through the woods, which before the great frosts of 1964 were a favourite haunt of green woodpeckers. Their tapping used to echo through the woods, giving the impression of foresters at work. When the road emerges from the trees, it runs beside the wood with a view across the valley towards the Salt Way at Roel Gate. The road wanders on, up and down the hills, through Brockhampton Park, with the village below, and then through Sevenhampton down to Syreford. Sevenhampton is a small group of well-kept buildings beside the stream, the recognized source of the River Coln. The church was enriched under the will of John Camber and there is a brass to him and plates to the Laurence family who lived in the Manor House for more than 300 years. The garden of the house spreads into the churchyard and, even in mid December, this sheltered spot was a riot of colour, with winter-flowering cherry, richly scented yellow mahonias, and roses having their final show of blooms before Christmas.

Whittington has some of the rarest sixteenth-century cottages, small and compact, with thick walls and heavy tile-stones. The Court, an unfortified manor house, was built on an older site, probably by Richard Cotton, who, according to a brass in the church, died in 1556. It was discovered that the Court stood on the site of a Roman villa. In the church, the ancient stone effigies of the thirteenth-century de Crupes family, possibly Crusaders, make one wonder if this site had been inhabited since the Romans left it. Like so many Cotswold churches it is immediately behind the manor house and both the house and the Tudor stables are best seen from the lane.

Towards Cheltenham, a steep lane leads up to Dowdeswell, with a view of the farms, manor house and

Shipton Solers. The ford across the River Coln. The Shiptons are pre-Saxon settlements, the name deriving from the sheep farms and pens, which belonged to the Abbot of Gloucester and the Bishop of Worcester

church, beautifully set on the side of the hill. Far below, fed by the River Chelt, is the wide expanse of Dowdeswell Reservoir. The wood behind is said to be haunted by the ghost of the last shepherd hanged for sheep stealing.

Lord Conway bought Sandywell Park at Dowdeswell in 1712. When his cousin, Horace Walpole, was his guest, he described the house as "a square box of a house, dirtily situated". Since then, many of the drives in the park have been given handsome gates, beautifully designed in wrought iron; these were added after Walpole's visit. Many of the Dowdeswell buildings are of stone from Whittington quarry, with tile-stones from Brockhampton and timber from Dowdeswell woods. Many well-wooded walks connect Dowdeswell with Colesbourne along the Hilcot valley, where there is one of the few timber-framed farmhouses remaining in the Cotswolds.

Two main roads loop through Andoversford on either side of the railway line. This was a small Roman town with some temples which, when ruined, became overgrown by the woods. The turnpike toll-keeper's house has been converted into a stone cottage. When turnpikes were first used on the Gloucestershire roads in 1747, the coaches from Gloucester to Oxford passed through Shipton. The Frogmill Inn was the first important staging post on the Gloucester to Oxford run. The Shiptons are low-lying, beside a small stream which flows into the River Coln. The Domesday Book and medieval records mention the locality as Froggemarshe or Frogmere. In 1086 the mill ground corn, and later ale was brewed there for the village feastings. Parts of the old mill are still visible at the inn, which was described by Samuel Rudder in his *New History of Gloucestershire* (1779) as "A good inn called Frogmill on the east bank of the Coln". Today's customers would agree with Rudder.

An outstanding feature of St Oswald's Church at Shipton Oliffe is the thirteenth-century open bellcote, showing its bells and wheels. The manor house, restored by Norman Jewson, has a large garden with formal water gardens, at times open to the public. St Mary's at Shipton Solers is a small thirteenth-century church standing above a long row of seventeenth-century stabling, facing across the yard to the manor house. The farm opposite is a mixture of ancient and modern. It has a large stone barn with two columns supporting a stout oak beam. In the straw, a sow and her piglets slept, undisturbed by the noise from the tall metal grain-dryer.

Christ rending the jaws of Satan. One of the six thirteenth-century bosses found in the chapter house of Hailes Abbey— on view in the museum

The Coln valley

CHAPTER SIX

Coln Valley to Cirencester

One of the joys of the Cotswolds is the rapidly changing scene. The country to the south-east of Northleach is quite different from the woods and Roman settlements around Chedworth. The lane through Mile End climbs the hill, crosses Helen's Ditch and leads to the sheltered Coln valley.

There are no tourist attractions on the way except for the countryside itself, which at the end of January had its own particular attraction. The lane which passes Cricklow Barrow and crosses the Salt Way on its way up to Roel Gate is high and open, but the earth in the ploughed fields is a richer red than the more usual limestone fields. The alders were purple with catkins and the yellow lamb's-tails of the hazels were swinging in the breeze. The Coln waters rise on Cleeve Hill, though Sevenhampton is the recognized source of the river, and from there it wanders through Withington and round the Chedworth Woods, joined by several other small brooks, and then flows down the Coln valley to Fairford, flowing eventually into the Thames at Lechlade.

The narrow walled lane drops steeply to the small village of Coln St Denis, with its low thatched barns, its original Norman church and a small stream beside the green. After crossing the bridge over the River Coln, the lane follows the course of the river, running beside the water meadows to Coln Rogers. Along the path to the Saxon church, a small paddock was white with snowdrops and there were drifts of them among the tombstones. Many of these were carved with a cherub's head and acanthus leaves, a design frequently found in Cotswold churchyards. Inside the church of St Andrew is a rare medieval oak chest with the original ironwork. The winter sun was shining on the seventeenth-century Pigeon House across the river, lighting up the grey stone façade, the flocks of fantails, the brilliant line of the flaming orange branches of willow trees kept neatly pollarded and catching the purple of the woods behind the house. While stopping to gaze at this feast of colour, a friendly donkey came to nuzzle my cold hands and a heron rose from his fishing at the water's edge.

"Starts slow and flaps his melancholy wing," John Clare wrote, but 'melancholy' is the wrong word; it is a leisured and dignified flight. Farther along, the Coln was

109

in flood, barely clearing the parapet of the low stone bridge at Ablington, a hamlet of Bibury. The road was the best way up to the long barrow, as the field paths were sodden, but in dry weather there are good walks over the Ablingdon Downs across to the River Leach or down into Bibury. Along the banks of the Coln, some farm children had seen a fox's brush hanging out of a hole in the river bank. One lay flat on the grass, leaned perilously over the edge, head nearly in the river, and daringly pulled the tail. No snarling fox turned on us; the brush came away in his hand and judging by the appalling stench, the fox had been dead for some time. The children proudly waved the brush, which was in fair condition and asked why the fox had died in the hole before he had time to take his brush in with him.

The houses in Ablington are privately owned. The Manor, built in 1590, was the home of J. Arthur Gibbs, who wrote one of the earliest books about the Cotswolds—*A Cotswold Village*, published in 1898. It is delightfully written and it is interesting to compare his impressions with the country as it is today. Proud of their author, one of the villagers boasted that Arthur Gibbs "said summat every time 'ee spoke". Ablington Manor was built by John Coxwell according to the inscription on the porch—

110

Plead thou my cause, Oh Lord,
John Coxwell Ano Domeney 1590.

Beneath are five carved heads, thought to represent Henry VIII, Mary and Philip of Spain, Elizabeth I and James I, so we are left in some doubt as to what John Coxwell's cause might have been.

The Manor was the later home of the Rev. Charles Coxwell, a vicar of Bibury for three years in the eighteenth century, a kind man who cared for orphans, paid for children's school books and provided extra food at Christmas. He was a merciful magistrate, reluctant to convict the local poachers searching desperately for their families' food. When he was Rector of Barnsley, he allowed the Welsh drovers, driving their huge flocks along the Welsh Way at nearby Ready Token, to spend the night in the Rectory grounds.

Opposite the Coxwell Manor at Ablington are two barns, one with five bays, larger than many a Cotswold church; the extension, with four bays, has a date-stone 1727. From the lane which leads down into Bibury, "we get a view we would gladly have walked twenty miles to see", wrote Arthur Gibbs. There is also a bird's-eye view of the extensive trout hatchery with its pools, fed by the River Coln. These hatcheries were started in 1906 by

Coln St Denis at the head of the Coln valley. The church of St James is
a rare example of unaltered Norman architecture

Coln Rogers, lower down the valley. The church of St Andrew boasts a Saxon nave and chancel

Arthur Severn, a cousin of John Ruskin. Arthur was the son of intellectual parents and grandson of Joseph Severn, a devotee of the poet John Keats—he was accompanying Keats when the latter died in Rome. Arthur was the black fish of this intellectual family, for the trout hatcheries were his principal interest until his death in 1949. The mill buildings changed hands several times after his death, until they were bought and restored by David Verey, the architectural historian.

A car park has been provided by the National Trust to enable visitors to Bibury to enjoy its beauty, visit the trout hatcheries and the mill, and to walk along the river to the cottages known as Arlington Row, originally a timber-frame wool hall faced with stone. The present cottages mostly date from the seventeenth century and were the homes of the weavers who supplied cloth to Arlington Mill. There it went through the 'fulling' or degreasing process, which consisted of treating the cloth in a suspension of fuller's earth, a clay-like substance derived from felspar which has the property of absorbing grease. Deposits of fuller's earth are found in many parts of the Cotswolds. Arlington Row was admired by Pope, enthusiastically described by William Morris and later by Arthur Gibbs. The cottages are small, have steeply pitched roofs and are set against a background of trees, with the water meadow and the river in front. The meadow is

Ablington, home of the author J. Arthur Gibbs

called Rack Isle, for it was here the cloth from the mill was hung on racks to dry. The meadow is preserved as a sanctuary and nesting ground for the water-fowl of the Coln, but on the side away from the river, there is a public footpath leading to the mill. The existing mill buildings are approximately seventeenth century, but a mill was recorded on the site in the Domesday survey. At that time, the place name was Bechberie and the lands and the church were held by St Mary's Priory at Worcester. They passed in 1130 to the abbey of Osney, near Oxford, and in spite of an attempt by the Bishop of Worcester to recover the lands, the claim was dismissed by King Henry II.

The mill was primarily used for grinding corn, but during the cloth boom the work of fulling was also undertaken, until the cloth industry moved to the Stroud valleys. After David Verey had restored the mill buildings, he opened them as a folk museum. The original grind stones can be seen on the first floor and although the machinery had been scrapped when Arthur Severn bought the mill, Mr Verey has replaced it with machinery of a similar type, now driven by an electric motor—thus visitors may see a working mill. The other rooms are full of interesting exhibits—agricultural implements of all kinds, a coracle boat, Roman coins and even a period dog-collar which belonged to a Bibury lady. In the miller's cottage, a bedroom has been furnished in the style of 1906, when Arthur Severn first bought the mill. Here, there is a water colour by his Uncle Walter. In the exhibition room are examples of the Arts and Crafts Movement, particularly of the Sapperton Group; fine pieces of furniture by Ernest Gimson, his chief craftsman Peter Waals and by Sidney Barnsley. The mill is open every day from 11.30 to dusk. In Bibury cemetery is a noteworthy tombstone in memory of a local farmer, father of Mr Verey's caretaker. It was worked by the young Cotswold sculptor Simon Verity and incorporates in the design all the tools and fruits of a farmer's work. Mr Verey also commissioned a fountain by the same sculptor for his own garden at Barnsley House.

So many visitors to Bibury see the mill, the hatcheries, Arlington Row and miss the village of Bibury further up the river. Here, the houses are grouped by the church, which has many signs of Saxon building, including two pilaster strips. These are clearly decorated with the Saxon interlacing circle and pellet design and have been placed on the north wall of the chancel. Many of the elaborate table tombs in the churchyard are those of the wealthy clothiers of the seventeenth century. A door in the churchyard leads into the orchard garden of the Bibury Court Hotel, open to non-residents. This gabled manor house beside the River Coln dates from Tudor times but the main portion was built by Thomas Sackville in 1633, with the arms of the Sackvilles over the porch. Sir Thomas was a Gentleman-Usher to King James I and the house was popular with royalty in the days of the Bibury Races. Charles II and the Prince Regent both stayed there. After the Sackvilles, the house passed to the Cresswells, who suffered from a disputed will and years of litigation; eventually the house was purchased by Lord Sherborne. It was on the records of the court case that Charles Dickens is said to

Bibury, Arlington Row. The seventeenth-century cottages were once used by weavers

have based his novel *Bleak House*. The walks through the grounds extend to the stone bridge over the Coln, with a path leading up through the woods. Refreshments are served on the terrace, which enables visitors to enjoy the beautiful setting. The main lounge is handsomely panelled and many of the bedrooms are furnished with four-posters.

I had been invited by David Verey to see the fountain by Simon Verity at his home, Barnsley House, but the rain came down in torrents. Sheltering under the trees of Coneygar Wood, I watched a stoat hypnotizing a rabbit. The rabbit, four times as large as the stoat, was completely powerless to move, as the stoat, crouching flat on the ground, stared at it, immobilizing it with fear. I chased it off but had to stamp my foot near the rabbit to wake it up and send it on its way.

There was a meet of the Vale of the White Horse Hunt that day on the lawn at Barnsley Park. The crossroads at Ready Token on the Roman Akeman Street were cluttered with horse-boxes. I was envying the horsemen their ride through the woods surrounding Barnsley until I had a puncture and discovered the cause was a horse-shoe nail. In a deluge of rain, I changed the back wheel, and wondered how John Keble, who knew the Cotswolds so well, could have written: "A gracious rain, refreshing the weary bower".

Over the hedge came some of the stragglers from the hunt, followed by a sporting parson. The unexpected sight of me startled the horses and nearly unseated the parson as he simultaneously raised his topper, regretted his inability to stop and rushed the opposite hedge. One Cotswold vicar was out with the hunt when the fox took refuge in an empty grave; he refused to allow the hunt to enter the churchyard on the grounds that the fox had claimed sanctuary.

A labourer, well protected by a large blue polythene sack, cycled past me and shouted: "Don't ee stay wet now, there's a good fire at the Greyhound." Taking his advice, I dried off in the warmth of the bar, helped by some hot ginger wine. John Tame, sponsor of Fairford church, once had a house on the site of the Greyhound, where he stayed to break his journey from Rendcombe to Fairford.

Opposite the inn, the rain was rushing down a Catslide roof, so aptly named by the cottagers, whose roof goes in one long steep slope from the ridge tiles to the edge of an outhouse. It splashed on a portly and parcel-laden housewife as she tried to squeeze through a stone V-shaped entrance to a footpath. I decided it was far too wet a day to ask Mr Verey to turn on his Simon Verity fountain at Barnsley House.

But Cotswold storms are often local, and on the downs on the east side of Bibury the sun was shining. The famous Bibury Racecourse was on these downs; the races were thought to have been inaugurated by John Dutton, owner of the Sherborne estates, in 1618. He coursed greyhounds on the downs and built Lodge Park beside the River Leach as a hunting lodge. The grandstand was near the present Macaroni Downs Farm and the course ran in a loop north-westward. Macaroni was the nickname for the foppish dandies who patronized the races.

Aldsworth was a bustling village in the days when George IV came to Bibury Races, invariably leaving without honouring his bets. Nothing is left of the old racecourse since the racing moved to Cheltenham and the stables are now converted into cottages. Aldsworth's church, together with that of Bibury, was the property of the abbey of Osney from 1130 to the Reformation and it still retains many Norman features. On the exterior of the church over one of the windows is a shield bearing the arms of the abbey of Osney, protected by a remarkable group of boldly sculptured grotesques, who glare down on all comers, good or bad. Aldsworth Downs were divided into fields by the eighteenth-century enclosure acts and new farmhouses were built with enormous barns. On Akeman Street is Sheephill Barn with its three bays, and the long cowshed, which has thirteen bays supported by eleven stone columns.

Across the fields past Blackpits Copse is Camp Barn, a hill-fort, with a view across to Macaroni and Woeful Lake Farms, the wood Snowbottom Belt, Cocklebarrow and Swyre Farm. This small estate, comprising a farmhouse, farm buildings and nine acres of land, was purchased and endowed in 1971 by a group of trustees as a Beshara centre for those wishing to study the teachings of the poet Rumi, in order to develop their potential to the full and give of their best to the world. Since the Whirling Dervishes first performed in Europe in 1971, many Westerners will have heard of Rumi, a thirteenth-century Muslim poet, scholar and mystic. The Dervishes are members of the Mevlevi, an ancient Muslim Sufi sect who celebrate the death of Mevlana Jalai'uddin Rumi with a religious ceremony at Konya in Turkey each December. The gyrating dance comes at the climax of the ceremony—a spectacle of dignified praise and worship.

> Come, come, whoever you are,
> Wanderer, worshipper . . .

These are Rumi's words and the welcome at any of the Beshara centres, where the general principles require that "Whatever work we are involved in, whether it is carpentry or study, the most important aspect is the degree of responsibility and awareness we put into it." It is an age-old doctrine and those staying at Swyre Farm adopt it

117

with the utmost sincerity. The centre can accommodate fifty comfortably and up to one hundred if necessary. People may stay for a day, a weekend or a year, so long as they comply with the way of life laid down in the daily rules, necessary for the running of any community. It was obvious that those who had stayed at Swyre during the last three years had worked hard to make the derelict farmhouse and buildings habitable. A granary had been converted into a library and the large cruciform barn into a place for prayer. The wind blew through the old tilestone roof, so they had constructed a dome above the centre section of the temple—an interesting structure based on the principles of sacred geometry. There was a good supply of blankets handy to protect the worshippers from the side draughts coming from the stone walls, still in need of pointing.

These earnest, dedicated young people seemed perhaps to lack a sense of humour. Joan Murray Simpson offers good advice.

> We might say to them, lean lightly,
> Don't burden a feeling
> With more weight than it can hold.

Beyond their boundary, by a neighbouring farm gate, was some cryptic Cotswold humour. A notice attached to a tree at the edge of an inviting but private wood read: "If bitten by an adder, go to Cirencester Hospital."

At Coln St Aldwyns, the approach to the church is spoiled by the ugly school building and the long, flat façade of the Memorial Cottages built in 1946. Nearer the river and the corn mill, the village is attractive, with cottages grouped around the green. The River Coln compensates for any architectural disappointments, as it flows through the water meadows beside the road to Williamstrip Park. The road goes through this park with its fine old trees, passing Hatherop Castle, now used as a school. The adjoining church and the castle were rebuilt by Lord de Mauley in 1854, in a French Gothic style, grand but rather foreign in their Cotswold setting.

The Ampney villages have quiet streets, lined with beautifully weathered stone houses under the trees beside the Ampney Brook. The ancient church of St Mary stands (or rather leans) alone, in a field beside the brook— the village has moved further up the hill. The church is small, with a rare lintel over the north door. The twelfth-century sculptor gave of his best to depict the Lion of Righteousness aided and abetted by a gryphon trampling over the evil spirits. Inside the church are the remains of a stone screen and some signs of wall paintings, which date from the twelfth to the fifteenth century. The narrow earth path to the church skirted a field of well-grown winter wheat, where a family of young rabbits were busy reducing the crop.

At Ampney St Peter, the small church is Saxon and was obviously rather damp, for cassocks were draped over the radiators. No one as yet has been able to identify the stone carving of a king holding an orb, which now rests on one of the windowsills, after being dug up on a local farm some years ago. But the carved stone head of the smiling lady in the tower has a definitely Saxon look. The close proximity of the Ranbury Ring and of the Iron Age fort, which encloses 20 acres, indicates a pre-Saxon settlement and adds to the feeling of great age which one senses both in this village and at Ampney Crucis, the largest of the Ampney villages. It is protected from the main road by the grounds of Ampney Park, which in Elizabethan times belonged to the Pleydell family. The beautiful gardens of the park slope down to Ampney Brook and are opened to the public on several days during the summer months.

The church of the Holy Rood is full of interest but the village is best known for the churchyard cross. The gabled head, with carvings of St Lawrence with his gridiron, *circa* 1415, was found walled up in the church and was only restored to the cross in 1860. During the Civil War, many of the clergy were afraid to record the deaths of soldiers fighting for either side. Not so Benedict Grace, Vicar of Ampney Crucis in 1644. He buried Jonas Graveline and

Ampney Crucis. The gabled head of the churchyard cross

119

Cirencester. This 'Capital of the Cotswolds' has been important since Roman times and was a centre of the wool trade for seven centuries

Adam Maritime, soldiers of the king. Grace was a royalist sympathizer, described by his parishioners in a long list of adjectives as quarrelsome, ignorant, lecherous, drunken and abounding in wickedness.

The large parish includes the ancient manors of Wiggold and Sheephouse, now farmhouses but once in the possession of Tewkesbury Abbey. On the Fosse Way near Wiggold is an old turnpike tollhouse.

At Ampney Riding, by a wood which stands beside the Roman Akeman Street, I leaned on a gate, looking back across the villages to the ancient hillfort and wondered what the people were like who for centuries past had worked on the land which lay before me, and what travellers had used the Roman road behind me. I munched my apple until a grey pony came nuzzling up and finished the remains. On leaving, I noticed some fading writing on the dilapidated field gate, which was tied to its post with a piece of rope. It read: "Tie a reef knot, the grey pony can untie a grannie."

One used to enter Cirencester bewildered by traffic signs, one-way streets cluttered with shoppers' cars, and eventually arrive at the large Forum car park, named after the Roman forum which once occupied the site. Now the splendid ring road is completed, circling the town outside the original Roman boundary wall. Clearly signposted, this relieves the narrow town streets of the through traffic.

Like all historic towns, Cirencester is best explored on foot. The car park is beside the Georgian Market Place, with its mellow stone façades above the shops, and this makes an excellent starting point. Here the most distinguished building is the magnificent three-storey porch of the church of St John the Baptist. Right on the pavement, amid the throngs of shoppers and bus queues, the porch dominates the Market Place as it has since the abbots added it to the church in 1500. The two storeys above the porch served as abbey offices and this is the only building of its kind in the country. After the Dissolution, when the abbey itself was completely destroyed, the upper floors of the porch continued in use as Town Hall offices, until the setting up of the Urban District Council.

An illustrated guide lists all the treasures within the church, but after a walk round sit and look up at the fine fan-vaulted roof, the carvings of angels supporting the heraldic shields of citizens of the town, the battle-scarred flags from Waterloo and the Peninsular War, look forward to the old chapels with their fifteenth-century glass windows and the excellent modern glass by Raston, Hardman and Kemp. The delicate wine-glass pulpit, carved in the fifteenth century, is one of the few of its type remaining in England.

The chapel of St John the Baptist is used as the choir vestry and opposite the handsome monument to George

Monox (a Sheriff of London in the reign of Charles I) was a blackboard. Some young choirboy had covered it with a picture in coloured chalks. Uninhibited by art school training, he had drawn the Three Kings charging towards the Star of Bethlehem on strange beasts, a cross between a camel and a horse. Lying beside the blackboard was a beautifully made corn-dolly cornucopia, forgotten by a flower arranger.

After absorbing the glories of the church, a walk in the abbey gardens immediately behind makes a welcome contrast to the bustle of the street. The College of Prebendaries was enlarged into a monastic abbey by Henry I, under a Norman abbot with the King as patron. The King, as Lord of the Manor of Oakley (now Cirencester Park), helped to provide a parish church for his people; this was the original of the present building. The abbey bought the Oakley Manor from Richard I, became rich and powerful, and by the Middle Ages controlled all the town's flourishing trade. Cirencester was the great market of the south Cotswolds and continued to be managed by the abbots, without a charter, borough status, or a merchant's guild, until the time of the Dissolution. Besides accumulating wealth, the abbots in 1458 founded a grammar school and developed a big trade in sheep, wool and cloth, with mills on the River Churn. It was the wealthy town merchants who founded the Hospital of St John in Spitalgate and the

twelfth-century almshouse, Weavers' Hall in Thomas Street.

On the orders of Henry VIII, nothing was to remain of the abbey. The treasures and dressed building stones were to be sold and the abbey privileges distributed among the local people, high and low. From a seat in the gardens visitors may see an ancient mulberry tree, 'The Abbot's Tree', which still survives on its many crutches, a Norman arch, and the gateway house to the Augustinian monastery, which stood on the site from 1117 to 1539. On the eastern side of the gardens is a section of the Roman wall, recently excavated and repaired. For those interested to learn something of the Roman city of Corinium Dobunni, start in the excellent museum in Park Street, with the archaeological museum next door.

The Roman Fosse Way was constructed about A.D. 47. It ran from Devon to Lincoln, crossing the intervening Cotswold escarpment. Patrolling troops were stationed at forts along the Way and the one at Cirencester occupied the land south of The Avenue. In A.D. 75, a town was founded beside the River Churn to serve as the administrative centre of the British Cotswold tribe, the Dobunni. Prior to this, their nearest centre was at Bagendon, overlooking the river valley three miles to the north. After the Dobunni had accepted Roman rule, they were expected to live in Roman style and the new city was called Corinium

Dobunnorum. It was the largest town at that time, only exceeded in size by Londinium's extra acres. Plans in the museum show clearly all the developments of the city.

Indirectly, the Romans are to blame for today's traffic problem, since they constructed three great highways which caused their Corinium to be known as 'The Cross-roads of Britain'. The Fosse Way, Ermin Street and Akeman Street all entered Corinium, whose ramparts were two miles in circumference, faced with local stone and entered by four main gates. Although much excavation has been carried out over the years, there are few Roman remains to be seen, though Lewis Lane and Watermoor Road were part of their street grid system. North-west of the new ring road, outside the old Roman walls, was the amphitheatre developed during the second century. Here were held the gladiatorial combats and fights with beasts. Now known as the Bullring, its grass-covered banks still stand 27 feet high and can be reached by a footpath west of the railway bridge in Cotswold Avenue.

Conquests, wars and centuries of haphazard building have left the town as we see it today; yet some of the older narrow streets are full of interest. Dollar Street, whose name intrigues American visitors, is a shortened version of Dole Hall Street, where the wealthy abbots distributed their largesse to the poor. The Market Cross is sheltered by

Dollar Street, Cirencester

a widely spreading blue-cedar tree, in a corner behind the church porch. The flat front of the Weavers' Hall, with its small windows, is in Thomas Street, the headquarters of flourishing craftsmen until the cloth industry finally moved north in the nineteenth century. Coxwell Street is as yet unspoilt; on one side are the houses of the wool-staplers, on the other, the humbler cottages of their workers. Castle Street has some typical seventeenth-century gabled houses and in Silver Street is the Georgian door-way of Campden House.

123

Cirencester Park, as seen from Duntisbourne Rouse

After all the interest of the town streets, there is the peace and beauty of the park, to be explored on foot or on horseback. After the rush of traffic, it is a relief to find that no vehicles are allowed in the park. The house is the present home of the Bathursts and was rebuilt from a previous Elizabethan house in 1718. Like the church porch, it is actually in the town and only protected from the road by a stone wall and a 30-foot high matured yew hedge. The back of the house faces towards Sapperton and the wide five-mile ride between is lined with trees.

In 1718, the Earl of Bathurst moved in an intellectual circle and many of his friends advised him on his rebuilding project—Lord Burlington on the architecture and interior decor and Alexander Pope on the planting of the trees in the park. Little is known of Lord Burlington's education, but he was certainly an amateur architect and after his 'Grand Tour' of Italy became an admirer of Palladio's architectural genius. This we see at his London home, Burlington House in Piccadilly, and better still at Chiswick House. In Italy he met, befriended and took into his house William Kent, whom Walpole described as "the father of modern gardening". So, with Steel, Gay and Congreve among his guests, the Earl of Bathurst had many witty advisers. Although the tree planting is attributed to Pope, one cannot help feeling that William Kent's advice was taken for the design of the magnificent vistas and general layout of the park. Established now for 200 years, it is a delightful place in which to walk under the avenues of elms and chestnuts and see the maples and cedars and the more decorative trees near the fine colonnaded house. Here spare another thought for the Romans, who introduced so many trees to Britain, including the pear, the cherry, the chestnut and the sycamore.

Most walkers in the country must wonder when a coppice becomes a wood and a wood a forest. Pope's words to Lord Bathurst are more amusing than the Oxford dictionary—

> Woods are—not to be too prolix,
> Collective bodies of straight sticks.
> It is my lord, a mere conundrum,
> To call things woods for what grows under 'em,
> For shrubs, when nothing else at top is,
> Can only constitute a coppice . . .

The general public is invited to enjoy Lord Bathurst's park from dawn till dusk.

Highly modernized farming and forestry work goes on there too which may be inspected by interested parties on application. Beyond the park is the Royal Agricultural College, founded in 1845 by a group of farmers to rescue the Cotswold farms from the decline in agriculture and the final loss of the wool trade. Its original research and teaching has strongly influenced farming practice. Every kind of research is carried out to improve soil, pasture, livestock breeding and veterinary science. The accommo-dation for students has increased from 90 to 700 and the agricultural advisory section offers a comprehensive ser-vice to farmers. Viscount Bledisloe, a former student and a governor of the college, offers a cup each year for the best-kept Cotswold village.

Bibury. The road bridge leads to Arlington Mill, built about 1770. The village of Bibury surrounds the Saxon church of St Mary and lies behind Arlington Row

CHAPTER SEVEN

Cleeve Common to Daglingworth

Breathless we flung us on the windy hill,
Laughed in the sun and kissed the lovely grass.
(Rupert Brooke)

Cleeve Common and Cleeve Cloud, the highest part of the long Cotswold escarpment, stretching for two miles, above 1,000 feet, is ideal walking or riding country, particularly on a clear, calm day. It is the largest uncultivated part of the wolds, being mainly 'gruffy ground', the remains of shallow stone diggings. Approach roads from several directions enable a car to reduce some of the worst of the uphill struggle, but quite rightly, cars are not allowed beyond the quarry car park by the golf house, from which the paths lead right across the glorious heights of the Cloud and the Common to the valley of the River Chelt. This is a wild, rugged walk, past many small quarry workings long since covered with the rough tufted grass which flourishes up there. A longer but less exposed walk is through the woods behind Postlip Hall and Corndean Hall, past Breakheart Plantation, well-named, as faint-hearted walkers turn back at this point. For those with plenty of stamina, the path eventually comes out on to the Common, at the head of Padcombe Bottom.

The young are well served by a youth hostel on the Cheltenham side. The back door of the house opens right on to the Common, with its wind-swept grasses. On a warm day, there is nothing more blissful than to lie in the tufty grass, like Margaret Rhodes seeing nothing but sky,

And larks above all—larks singing their hearts out
The sky trembling with song.

Here, the ramblers stride along part of the Cotswold Way, as it reaches the Cloud beside the youth hostel. The Way skirts the golf course, passes behind Castle Rock and the earthworks of Hill Fort, and crosses the Common at the highest point—1,082 feet above sea level—before descending to the villages of Whittington and Dowdeswell.

The source of the River Thames is claimed to be in several places and one of these is in what used to be a quiet dell called Seven Springs. Since the construction of a large road roundabout, it is poorly signposted and easily missed. It lies to the right of the A436 to Gloucester, just after it crosses the A435. The small dell is surrounded by stately beeches; there are rough steps down to the springs. This source of our mighty Thames, here called the River Churn, is a rather small damp patch at the foot of a stone wall. The wooden signposts on the site are beautifully lettered with incised gold, but difficult for the passing motorist to read. The curved road behind the site provides adequate parking for visitors.

The A435, after climbing up into the hills, follows the Churn valley into Cirencester and the countryside is equally beautiful on either side of the road. On the right, down the lane to Coberley, adjoining the present Court House, is the archway to Coberley's vanished Hall, its keystone a smiling stone head. The Hall was one of the many homes of the Berkeleys and the small church stands beyond the house yard; it contains some of the tombs of the Berkeley family. Dick Whittington was the son of Sir William Whittington of Pauntley; his father became a poor man when he married, without licence, the widow of Sir Thomas Berkeley. Selling rich widows was a lucrative perquisite of the Crown. Sir William was outlawed until he had paid the crippling fine for his redemption.

Richard, the third son, lived happily enough at Coberley Hall and at Pauntley until he had to leave to enrol as prentice with the Mercers' Company. True to pantomime tradition, he certainly married Alice Fitz-Warren, his master's daughter, and was thrice Lord Mayor of London, in 1397, 1406 and 1419. The effigy of his mother Joan is in Coberley church.

Beyond the hamlet of Coberley, the lane leads to the gateway of Cowley Manor, where the River Churn feeds the lakes. Adjoining the house is St Mary's Church, where Lewis Carroll's uncle was the Rector, and the original of Alice in Wonderland a frequent visitor. The church, like that at Coberley, is almost a part of the big house, for only the thick yew hedge separates them. The church, on the site of an earlier building, dates back to the thirteenth century: existing when the Manor of Cowley was given to the Abbey of Pershore by Edward the Confessor. The Manor, like that of Coberley, was leased to the great family of Berkeley, who owned so much of Gloucestershire.

The manor house has had many owners and undergone many alterations. The present house, which was largely altered in 1850 by Sir James Horlick, is now owned by the Gloucester County Council and is used as a residential conference house. Judging by the posters, it is a lively educational centre, keeping a close link with both the small village and the church.

To the west of Cowley, Birdlip is one of the last heights of the long Cotswold escarpment before it slopes gently down to Cirencester, Stroud and The Bottoms. I can never pass Birdlip without parking my car with the other tourists and gazing in wonder at the view across the Berkeley Vale and the Severn estuary to the Welsh hills. The remains of a deep quarry immediately below the parking line make the view even more dramatic, as the outcrop of warm stone, lit by a westering sun, eventually disappears among the acres of Cranham Woods. During the Roman occupation, Birdlip was a posting station, approached by their Ermin Way, as it is today. During the eighteenth-century coaching era, a road was made up through the steep wood from Witcombe Park to the Black Horse Inn, and a Turnpike House stood at the top of the hill. It was at the Black Horse that the now famous Cotteswold Naturalists' Field Club first met in 1846.

The queen of the Dobunni tribe ruled the area before the Romans and when Barrow Wake was excavated, a mirror and some jewellery were found in a grave thought to have been that of the queen. The Birdlip mirror, with many more of the barrow treasures, is in the Gloucester Museum.

On Birdlip Hill, Ermin Way crosses the old Calf Way, used in past centuries by the drovers taking their beasts to the Cotswold markets. Opposite Witcombe Wood is a good round walk, passing through Climperwell and bearing left through Caudle Green. At Haycroft, a cottage still retaining a moulded stone doorway is possibly the chantry chapel founded by Thomas Berkeley in 1344. The path crosses the lane to the small early Norman church at Syde and continues via Brimpsfield Park Farm over the Wind Rump back to Witcombe.

East of Birdlip are the ruins of Brimpsfield Castle, the home of the Giffard family. The manor was given to them by the Conqueror and Osbern Giffard became Lord of Brimpsfield in 1086. The ancient site is on private farming land, but the path across the fields to the church is a public right of way. From this path, the dry moat and the wide south entrance of the castle are clearly discernible. John Giffard was one of the barons who rebelled against Edward II, for which misdemeanour he was hanged and his castle demolished. The Giffards had a good water supply, for the River Frome rises under the castle mound. This is the only Cotswold river which flows into the Severn. After making its leisurely way south to Sapperton, it turns west, to flow along the Golden Valley. Frome water was used to power the many mills along the river banks. During the cloth boom, folk said the name 'Golden' referred to the golden guineas of the wealthy clothiers, not to the wealth of autumn colour which emblazons the valley woods.

An ancestor of John Giffard gave the church with a small grant of land to the Benedictine monastery at Fonteney in Normandy and this Order established a priory just north of the church. On the left of the path leading to the church is a small stone barn with a trefoil window and traces of the foundations of the priory. The public path passes under three wide yew archways to the fourteenth-century church porch, which protects the Norman doorway. The stone for the church and probably for the castle came from Smith's Cross quarry on Ermin Street, which used to produce the best walling stone in the Cotswolds. When the castle was demolished, the dressed stone was soon carted away by the local masons. One piece of stone decorated with four consecration crosses, thought to have been used as a communion table by the Giffards was found as part of a stile in 1937 and was restored to the church.

From the churchyard, which is 800 feet above sea level forming one side of the castle moat, there is a magnificent view of the gradual slope down towards Cirencester. From this height, the four towers of the old castle must have commanded a view across to the hills of Wales. On the walk back to the village, my thoughts were turned away from the fierce Giffards by the sight of a newly born Jersey calf being washed clean by its mother and nudged gently to get on its feet.

I continued on my zigzag way across the Roman Ermin Street to Elkstone. Of the many churches of Saxon and Norman origin in this district, the church of St John at Elkstone is the finest. The name of the village is Saxon and means 'the stone building of Ealac'. The stone against the wall in the vestry, with its non-Christian pattern, is believed to be extremely old and may be the stone which gave the village its name. The building dates from about 1160. The two human heads in the beakhead ornament of the beautifully preserved south door are thought to represent the founder, Richard of Cormeilles, and his wife. Much has been written about this little church, with its tower, its gargoyles, priest's house and pigeon loft, but you have to sit in it to appreciate to the full the two heavily carved Norman archways and the small window arch beyond. Of all the churches built by man to the glory of God, this small building must be unique.

After the heights of Elkstone, I returned to the Roman Ermin Street for the sheer pleasure of driving along the beautiful stretch of road called Gloucester Beeches. I left it at Beechpike and wandered through the wooded lanes to Colesbourne, to take the walk which skirts Colesbourne Park. There, the Hilcot Brook comes down from the upper wolds and joins the Churn. The house deep in the woods was the home of H. J. Elwes (1846–1922), Squire of Colesbourne, a soldier and traveller who made a particular study of lilies, rare plants and trees. He encountered enormous difficulties in the afforestation of the 700 acres of poor land and was badly hindered by the diseases which followed the disastrous season of 1879. However,

The church of St John, Elkstone. The two arches lead to the sanctuary of the original tower

his ecological experiments were some of the finest attempted in this country. He was a pioneer in the work of relating soil, water, nutrients and climatic factors to the establishment and management of forests. He published many books on his work and founded the quarterly *Journal of Forestry* in 1907. His seven volumes on *The Trees of Great Britain and Ireland* were published in 1913. He succeeded in establishing many rare trees at Colesbourne—the Californian nutmeg, the Japanese wingnut, the Chinese lime and the Turkish hazel. His golden western red cedars are now amongst the largest in the country.

Colesbourne Park owes much to this burly man with his sensitive appreciation of natural beauty. The road is particularly beautiful here, with the Penhill and Eycott Woods on the one side, on the other the valley of the Churn, as it leaves Colesbourne Park and flows through the flat meadows before being lost to view in the woods of Rendcombe Park.

At Withington I took the walk which crosses the manor garden between two stone walls, under arched overpaths. The sun was shining, the washing was laid out country fashion—spread on rosemary and lavender bushes. In the village street the old forge has been converted into a house. Admiring the view, my stay was shortened by the rooks which were nesting in the trees above. Even if you believe in the good luck theory of being splashed with bird droppings, no one wishes to become snow white. Withington is a site known to the Romans, the Saxons and the Normans. The Roman villa was destroyed by fire in the fourth century but there is much Norman work remaining in the restored church. Over 1,200 years ago, one of the earliest Cotswold monasteries was founded here by St Aldhem. In the fifteenth century, the bishops of Worcester owned the manor house, and Halewell Close was said to be their Great House.

At the bottom of the street, on the bend of the River Coln, which rises near Andoversford, are the Mill Inn and Mill House. These were largely rebuilt in 1960 from old stone recovered from Northleach prison. The well laid-out garden of the inn is a pleasant place for refreshments. Immediately beyond the track of the disused railway is a lane which runs through Withington Woods. Here the brown butterflies were mating on the wing and two cock pheasants were fighting in the centre of the road, like the fighting cocks of old, presumably for a hen watching from the top of a bank. From the high open ground at Chedworth Laines there is a gated road down into Rendcombe. The old Rendcombe Manor was the home at the beginning of the sixteenth century of Sir Edmund Tame, who, with his father, had been responsible for building the famous church at Fairford. St Peter's Church at Rendcombe was rebuilt by Sir Edmund in 1517.

The church contains some early wood carvings and tombs of the Berkeley and Guise families, who held the manor after the Tames. The Guise family was reputed to have brought the superbly carved Norman font from Elmore.

The manor house was rebuilt in 1661 by Sir Christopher Guise and again in 1863 by Sir F. H. Goldmid and is now a boys' college. The massive stable block is some way from the house, which accounts for the fine cast-iron bridge over the village road.

Lower down the valley at North Cerney, the church and the rectory are on one side of the road and on the other the Bathurst Arms, with the village rising up behind it in a fold of the hills. The beasts cut into the exterior stone work of All Saints' Church resemble the manticores described by Pliny, who believed they were to be found in Ethiopia—"the face and ears of a man . . . the body of a lion . . . and a tail ending in a sting, like that of a scorpion . . . and particularly fond of human flesh". The North Cerney drawings are dated approximately to the sixteenth century. Could this early Cotswold mason have heard of Pliny or seen a copy of a bestiary, or were they figments of his own imagination? Either way, he obviously enjoyed illustrating them in his stonework. On the right jamb of the doorway of the tower there is a clearly defined scratch dial or mass clock with only five radii. This usually indi-

cates a pre-Conquest date, but the south doorway is unmistakably Norman, with its diapered tympanum. Here again, an early mason enjoyed his work and carved four small human heads into the lintel—possibly those of his employers.

The porch, which has helped to preserve the doorway from the weather, has a timber roof of the fourteenth century, which may also be the date of the heavy wooden door, so beautifully carved with flowers in high relief. The modern visitor has reason to be grateful for the porch, which screens him from the wild Cotswold wind while examining the tympanum. In the churchyard, exposed to all the elements, is an unusual cross. The shaft and the steps are fifteenth century, but the head, in the form of an earlier Maltese cross, was discovered nearby and placed on the old shaft quite recently. Wild plantains, which as children we called grandmother's whiskers, were growing between the stone steps of the cross. I could not resist playing the childish game of firing the brown conical heads of the plantains by twisting the stem into a loop at the back, then pulling with a quick jerk to make the hard brown heads fly off in the direction of a victim.

As so often happens when you go in search of one treasure, you find another. I knew the interior of the church was full of antiquities—Norman capitals, Jacobean carvings, a medieval lantern and many other items of interest.

Duntisbourne Abbots. From the lychgate of St Peter's Church there is an excellent view of the valley of the Duntisbourne Brook

I was not expecting the well-designed clothes-press, which, the rector explained, solved the very real problem of storage in a small church with scanty vestry accommodation. This cypress-wood vestment press, with its two tall cupboards on either side of a set of drawers, the top of which served as a side-chapel altar, could have been a Gimson or a Barnsley piece. Although it was in their style, it was designed about 1928 by the ecclesiastical architect F. C. Eden and made by Cook, a well-known cabinet maker in Soho. The metalwork was by Hobbs, who made the porch gates, also designed by Eden.

I am always fascinated by coincidence. As I sat in the car with a hot drink, I opened my copy of *Concrete 98*, which happened to contain photographs of Picasso's experimental drawings in concrete. Those are now in the museum at Antibes and in the Government Buildings in Oslo are strangely reminiscent of the manticores I had just seen.

An adventurous, attractive route into Cirencester follows the Duntisbourne Brook as it flows through the three villages named after it. The lanes linking them are narrow, steep and winding, following the contours of the hills. Lane and brook frequently cross one another or share the same course between drystone walls, the only surviving water lane in the Cotswolds. At the head of the valley is Duntisbourne Abbots, a village of cottages and houses,

Duntisbourne Leer

centuries old, dominated by the Norman church of St Peter, where the churchyard literally overhangs the steep lane down to Middle Duntisbourne and Duntisbourne Leer. Here the fords once used for soaking cart wheels, are still used for washing horses' hooves. Duntisbourne Abbots was a possession of St Peter's Abbey, Gloucester, and Leer is named after the Normandy Abbey at Lire, to which it belonged before passing to Cirencester Abbey in 1416.

An engineer friend at Duntisbourne Abbots managed to buy the old wheelwright's shop, saw-pit, forge and two cottages, in which to spend his retirement. The wheelwright's shop is as it was left, except that a motor car now stands where once a cart or carriage stood awaiting repair. By the door is the original simple vice operated by a wooden handle, the item for repair being held by the sheer weight of a large piece of local stone. At the far end, rough stairs lead up to what the wheelwrights called 'the up and over'. On this gallery, the more delicate carriage repair work was handed up to the carpenter and painter. Outside is the ring of stones on which the wheels were placed for shaping and banding with iron rims. Opposite is the saw-pit (now a wood shed), where the top and bottom sawyers controlled the cutting, the top or master sawyer standing astride the log at ground level, guiding the cuts with the long two-handled saw. 'Bottom'

stood in the pit providing most of the manpower. It was gruelling, dusty work and 'Bottoms' were notorious drinkers. High-grade timber was sawn, giving a straight, clean edge. The present owner has the last plank cut in the pit—it is 10 feet long, the width of half an inch accurate throughout this length. Lower-grade timber was cleft, giving rough and wavy scantlings, frequently seen in rafters. Wattle staves and battens for tile or thatch were made from cleft timber. It is more durable than the sawn timber as it follows the grain and minimizes splitting.

The forge has been converted into the engineer's own workshop, where he follows his hobby of making miniature furniture—accurate reproductions made from carefully selected second-hand timber. One was a chest of drawers with an elegant serpentine front, about 10 inches by 6 inches, with perfectly sliding drawers and handmade minute metal handles, a useful container for small objects. The path to his converted cottages is lined with the old grindstones from the smithy.

St Michael's Church at Duntisbourne Rouse is so unobtrusive it could easily pass for one of the cottages if it were not for the signpost in the hedge and the small lychgate. A sloping path leads to a rare scissor-gate (one of the few remaining in England). At the entrance to the churchyard stands a fourteenth-century cross. The exterior walls of the church show large Saxon quoin stones, areas of herringbone masonry, and the nave appears to be Saxon. The sloping site was used to make a small crypt chapel, Norman in character, which is approached by an outside staircase. Inside, the fifteenth-century choir stalls have their original misericords and there are traces of wall paintings of the same period.

On the harmonium was a small card stating that it was given in memory of Katherine Mansfield by her sisters. Sitting at the edge of the churchyard, high above the small brook in the meadows below, I recalled the descriptive writing of Katherine Mansfield—" . . . there came the sounds of little streams, flowing quickly, lightly, slipping between the smooth stones, gushing into ferny basins . . ." It aptly described the valley below me, although 'At the Bay' was written about New Zealand. Katherine Mansfield (1888–1923) was a member of the Bloomsbury set, a friend of D. H. Lawrence and Middleton Murry. Her short and turbulent life was spent battling against ill-luck and ill-health, whilst writing her stories; she died of tuberculosis at the age of thirty-four. I had enjoyed her writing and was interested to be able to talk about her with her sister, living in retirement in the village. I heard at first hand about Queen's College in Harley Street, where she and her sisters were sent to be educated in 1902; about Katherine's final retreat after the war years, to Gurdjieff's Institute for the Harmonious Development of Man at Fontainebleau. It was here, in this sanctuary for unhappy intellectuals, that she had hoped to find health and peace, but she died before she found either. André Maurois considered her short stories had a similar quality to those of Checkhov and Maupassant.

On the hill to the west of Rouse are the Hoar Stone and a long barrow, known locally as Jack Barrow, in which

Duntisbourne Rouse

was found a stone chest and an early longsword. From Duntisbourne Rouse the lane passes through Dagling-worth, a village of delightful buildings, some of them grouped around the restored Saxon church while others are at Lower End. The ownership of this quiet little vil-lage has changed hands repeatedly since the time of the Saxon owners. In Henry VIII's reign it belonged to the Berkeleys, then to the Pooles of Sapperton—following them, Sir Robert Atkyn, the historian, then Lord Bathurst of Cirencester. Now it belongs to the Duchy of Cornwall and Prince Charles has recently subscribed to the Village Hall Fund. The notices on the boards of village halls often make amusing reading. One announcing a dance ended: "Dress optional. It may be a cold night."

In the grounds of Lower End House, built on an earlier site, the Godstow nuns left a fine medieval dovecote with a string-course to prevent rats climbing into its 500 nest holes. Rosamund the Fair was acknowledged by King Henry II as his mistress after the imprisonment of his Queen, Eleanor of Aquitaine. Many stories have been told about the King's great love affair, how Eleanor tried to poison Rosamund, who eventually took refuge with the nuns and was buried in the nunnery church of Godstow in 1176.

In the church of the Holy Rood are three rare late Saxon stone figures. They were found, set face inwards, serving as the jambs of the chancel arch. Earlier than the church, David Verey dates them about 1050. They are crude but sincere works respectively of the Crucifixion, St Peter, and Christ enthroned.

An early vice in use in the wheelwright's workshop in Duntisbourne Abbots

Painswick, a small hill town

CHAPTER EIGHT

Painswick to Sapperton Tunnel

Painswick with its buildings of grey stone from the local quarries, differs in many ways from the golden towns and villages further north. It developed as one of the important spinning and weaving centres rather than as a sheep-breeding, agricultural area. After the Conquest, the Manor of Wyke was given to Roger de Lacy. It was not until the early thirteenth century, when the manor belonged to Pain Fitzjohn, that it began to be called Pain's Wyke. Spinning and weaving developed as a cottage industry but the increase in cloth making was not really stimulated until the sixteenth century, when a colony of Flemish weavers settled there. They built fulling and finishing mills. Soon the cottages resounded with the noise of shuttles flying to and fro, as people of both sexes and all ages joined in the growing cloth boom. By 1820, thirty cloth mills were producing blue cloth for the navy, red and green for the army and black for wear on Sundays. Woad, a plant native to central and southern Europe, grew well around Painswick and was used to obtain a dense black, until superseded by the import of indigo in the reign of Queen Elizabeth I. Today, woad has become one of our rare wild flowers, difficult to find except in occasional places nearer the Severn. From seed sown in February, woad became a rank growth by summer. The blue-green leaves were picked four times from one sowing, giving between one and two tons per acre but leaving the ground useless for the following season, for woad is a ferocious feeder. The leaves were smashed to a pulp by a horse-powered grinder, the pulp was then rolled into balls, turned and watered. Only the neediest people worked on woad, for the stench was appalling. The ancient Britons must have become immune to this when they used it to paint their bodies, unless it was applied as the first insect repellent.

When fancy materials were introduced from France and Italy, requiring new machinery for ribbing and Jacquard weaving, the stubborn Cotswold folk refused to change their methods. Their business was steadily lost to the industrial north, with its sweated labour working up-to-date looms. Painswick, after much suffering and unemployment, settled down to be the quiet hillside, commuter town it is today. Here the Gloucestershire Guild of Craftsmen have their headquarters and hold their annual exhibition for three weeks each August.

The churchyard at Painswick is as famous as the church, for it contains the finest array of table tombs in the Cotswolds. They are mostly seventeenth and eighteenth century, designed in the Renaissance tradition by the expert stonemasons who were employed by the wealthy clothiers. The Bryans, a local family of stonemasons, were responsible for much of the rich carving. Joseph Bryan lived from 1682 to 1730 and it was his son John, who died in 1787, who designed a plain pyramid for his own tomb, a miniature of the Caius Cestias tomb in Rome, no doubt knowing how well it would stand out amongst the ornate tombs of the wealthy. For some years past, the townspeople have realized the unique value of the tombs and have formed a society for their preservation. By following the walk suggested on the numbered plan in their leaflet 'Tomb Trail', you see the finest of the Bryans's work and read the names of the famous clothiers—the Lovedays, the Tocknells, the Packers, the Pooles and the Pallings. These families, like the earlier wool merchants, built fine houses for themselves and good stone cottages for their weavers. It is these buildings which make Painswick such an interesting town in which to walk, or rather climb, for many of the narrow streets leading down to the river and up to the Beacon are steep.

The steeple of St Mary's Church dominates the town and its peal of twelve bells echoes down the valley towards Stroud. The two oldest bells were given in 1686. The New Church, as it was called in 1377, was erected by the prior and canons of Llanthony Abbey. Since that date it has had many alterations. It was severely damaged by the royalists in the Civil War, as they drove out the occupants with fire. In 1883, the spire was struck by lightning and much of the stonework fell through the roof.

Many reasons have been given for the origin of yew trees in churchyards. The yew was once known as the Funeral Tree: centuries ago, when these lines were written—

> . . . yon black and funeral yew,
> That bathes the charnel house with dew.

—mourners used to carry branches of yew, which they laid above and below the box or skin sack containing the body, to protect it from evil spirits, which they believed would not approach the poisonous yew. The yew was also regarded as a symbol of immortality and its red cupped berries as drops of blood. Yew wood was used for furniture, especially bedsteads, as it repelled bed bugs. Although it was known to be baneful to man and beast, the juice was administered to children as a cure for worms.

The elaborate table tombs in St Mary's churchyard, Painswick, are memorials to the town's wealthy citizens—"William Loveday, Yeoman, 1623" is the oldest inscription and "John Baylis, Clothier, 1818" more recent

Very few children or worms survived the dose. Yew was used to make the longbow, though a keen Cotswold archer maintains that ash is far better. The longbow was the most formidable weapon of the Plantagenet kings. Threatened by the advance of the Black Prince, whose bowmen had been victorious at Crécy and Agincourt, Spain stopped the export of seasoned yew to England. English farmers, who had known of the poisonous effect of yew on horses and cattle since the Roman Conquest, refused to plant them, in spite of the government's pressing demands. The problem was solved by planting them in country churchyards, in "God's Acre, where no cattle strayed".

The demand for the longbow ceased with the introduction of gunpowder in Tudor times. The yew tree then came into its own again when the art of topiary became fashionable with English gardeners at the beginning of the eighteenth century, largely due to John Evelyn, well known for his *Diary*. He also published several books on gardening, including *Sylva*, a valuable book on arboriculture. He was largely responsible for the re-afforestation which took place in England after the glass and iron works had denuded the countryside of its timber.

The yew trees at St Mary's, Painswick, were planted about 1792. There are reputed to be ninety-nine of them and no matter how often the hundredth is planted, it will not survive. They are kept architecturally clipped. In September, a respectable version of the ceremony of 'embracing the church' is revived—here it is called 'clipping the yews', a time when the congregation join hands in a ring around the church. Gone are the days when the rustic hymn singers brought with them a supply of ale, cider and the seductive maidens, garlanded with flowers, enticed them away for illicit love-making. Painswick, like many country places, suffered from drunkenness and debauchery as a result of the Cider Tax, which lasted for three years from 1763. It was so iniquitous to tax the home-brewed staple drink of the poor, that many farmers gave away their cider, rather than pay the tax. It was heaven help the poor excise man who tried to enforce it. Many are the tales of how the wily countryfolk dealt with them. Although they had to feed him, the miners of the Forest of Dean captured their man and kept him in their mine until the tax was repealed. For once, the landed gentry, the clergy and the sheriffs were on the side of the poor. After many rebellious meetings, ending in a mass meeting at the Booth Hall in Gloucester, the tax was abolished.

Before Painswick became a borough in 1253, Gloucester Street and Bisley Street were the main roads. After 1252, the town steadily developed, with the addition of New Street and many narrow lanes. There are several houses in New Street which were previously the homes of wealthy cloth manufacturers. Beside Cotswold House are the gate piers which lead to an early nineteenth-century warehouse. The Post Office is one of the few buildings showing exposed timbers; the Beacon and Hazlebury House are examples of the Palladian style. Hazlebury bears a Sun Insurance Company plaque relating to Daniel Packer's insuring of the house and cloth store with the company in 1757.

The Court House by the church was built in 1604 for a clothier named Thomas Gardner; the three-storey extension which has the Court Room on the first floor was built for Dr John Seaman, Diocesan Chancellor, who died in 1623. The Court Room may be viewed by the public.

From the small square, Tibbiwell Street leads down to Painswick Stream and the old mills, passing on the way the decorative façade of the Golden Heart. The street is so steep that some thoughtful person has provided a handrail. Tibbiwell is named after St Tabitha's well which in the sixteenth century was known as Towy's Well and it was forbidden to wash anything unclean in the spring which fed it. Many of the cottagers managed to keep a pig in their small gardens, under conditions which would horrify modern sanitary inspectors, but even in those days it was forbidden to wash their swine's entrails in the spring. At the bottom of the lane, where it crosses the stream, is Brookhouse Mill, one of the few remaining working mills, called a pin mill but making a variety of small metal components.

Turn right along King's Lane and you will see many of the old cloth mills, now converted into elegant houses and beautifully landscaped. The last one along the stream before it turns and flows down Painswick Valley, beside the main road into Stroud, is King's or Lower Mill. It is reputed to have been mentioned in the Domesday survey and there are records of a mill on the site in 1495, although its function is unknown. It was worked as a cloth mill by the Palling family until at least 1820, then as a cap mill and later as a pin mill until the 1900s. The outbuildings, comprising wool, teazle stores and drying rooms, have been demolished and an elegant L-shaped stone building remains. The rows of weavers' windows on the first floor light a long lounge on both sides, and the waters of the Painswick Stream, joined by Wash Brook, flow through the gardens.

In complete contrast to the low-lying King's Lane are the heights of Painswick and Haresfield Beacons. Painswick Beacon is an ideal place for children's games of hide and seek, as many tracks lead in and out of the bushes. For serious walkers, the Cotswold Way crosses the Beacon and all the paths are well signposted. Many walkers follow the example of Charles I, though in happier circum-

Paradise, near Painswick Beacon

stances, and find their way to the small wooded hamlet which the King described as 'Paradise'. This name seemed so apt for the district that it was adopted and the name of the Plough Inn was changed to The Adam and Eve. The conifers in the grounds of a future Paradise House are now said to have been brought from the Holy Land.

The houses scattered about the Beacons were mostly built by the clothiers and more recently modernized by other wealthy people whose businesses are not in Painswick. Painswick Lodge is perhaps one of the oldest houses—a hunting lodge dating from the thirteenth century and restored when Henry VIII brought Anne Boleyn to Painswick on one of their hunting trips. In 1928 it was restored by Sidney Barnsley and cottages were added by Norman Jewson—both architects of the Sapperton Group.

The Cotswold Way crosses the hills from Birdlip, over Coopers Hill (famous for its cheese-rolling festival), and across the heights of Painswick Beacon before dropping down into Painswick.

Over the hills and valleys to the east, past Jacks Green and Sheepscombe, is a small colony at Whiteways. I was privileged to have met that great pioneer character Nellie Shaw, a simple girl from Croydon, who tried to live out her life on the Cotswold Hills as a true follower of Tolstoy. In the 1890s, Tolstoy had many followers in England, living according to his philosophy—"building their own house, tilling their own land . . . and sharing all things in common". The many brotherhoods formed during the years by followers of Tolstoy collapsed either through lack of money or, as at Purleigh, because they were given too much by wealthy well-wishers.

Nellie Shaw and the Whiteway pioneers were determined to make Tolstoy's ideas work. They spent their savings on 42 acres of bare, hilly land, the limestone mud making white tracks across it, hence the name Whiteways. There were no trees on the land and only one small stone house, which for some years was the community's only refuge from the bitterly cold winters. The deeds of the land were burned, in true Tolstoy spirit, but it is still recognized as colony land. I last visited Nellie Shaw, the only survivor of the original Whiteway Colony, in 1945. She was over eighty but still a lively and witty conversationalist, living in the wooden shack which she and the Czech philosopher, Francis Sedlak, had built for themselves in 1901. In her book *Whiteways*, she writes of the failure of their true communism, their turning to individualism, their belief in free expression and free union. On that cold January day in 1945, I was driving slowly down the rough track which led to Nellie's home-made bungalow, when out of a neighbouring shack came a busy housewife carrying a large brown teapot. She walked across the frozen grass to empty the tea leaves on her compost heap. She was quite naked. I think it was the large brown teapot which made her look as if she had walked straight out of a French farce.

I prize a beautiful yew wood box, edged with black, which was given me that day by Fred Foster, a pupil of Sidney Barnsley. Though not one of the original members at Sapperton, he was a master craftsman and had been a member of the Whiteway Colony all his married life. Trees and hedges have since grown up to hide the shacks, which are now rented to suitable tenants. However many of the premises must be regarded as eyesores by the Country Planning Commission and one would imagine their future is in doubt. The bungalow built with unskilled care by Francis Sedlak and Nellie Shaw, where they enjoyed thirty years of free union, is occupied but is in need of vital reconstruction. There was an appetizing smell of Christmas cakes coming from the original Protheroe Bakery, but the young baker at work beside the cast-iron oven knew nothing of its origin.

A furniture maker and his wife, an excellent wood carver, were living in a shack beside the tarmac road which leads down the hill to Miserden. The shack had been the home of the carver's parents, leather workers and bookbinders, who had joined the Whiteways Colony in 1922. The present couple and their son were lively members of the Arts and Crafts Society. Their undaunted enthusiasm, their goats tethered in the untidy land at the rear, reminded me of Nellie Shaw, as I walked down the hill, past the stone house where she spent so many bitter winters with little to eat but turnips.

Nearby is that eye-catching folly, Hazle House, with its tall, three-storeyed central block crowned by magnificent stone eagles, also the sixteenth-century Wishanger Farm. Miserden is a trim unspoilt village. The tree in the square is not only encircled by a seat, but also by a tiled roof. It is a sheltered place from which to admire the woods of Miserden Park, which in Elizabethan and Stuart times was the home of the Sandys family. The old house has a new wing, designed by Sir Edwin Lutyens, and stands in a spectacular position facing the steep wooded valleys where the young waters of the River Frome meander among the trees. Many of the original Whiteway colonists are buried in Miserden churchyard and the drastically restored Saxon church contains some magnificent monuments. The effigies of Sir William Sandys and his wife, Margaret Culpepper, depicting every detail of their elaborate Stuart costumes, are carved in Derbyshire alabaster. The painted effigy of William Kingston (1614) rests his feet on a goat which is complacently eating a cabbage.

At the top end of the village are several blocks of

148

cottages designed by Sidney Barnsley in 1920 and built in true Cotswold style. A walk from Bull Banks, below Miserden Park passes through the glorious woods across to Duntisbourne Common and Edgeworth.

Most country children care for injured animals; when I called at a farm on the way to Bisley, a long-suffering mother had an injured heron perching on her clothes airer and a mangy stray cat sitting on a high shelf among her saucepans. The cat was keeping a wary eye on the heron and looked down on all comers, like the Cheshire puss in *Alice in Wonderland*. In the scullery her children showed me a small aviary they had been allowed to build for their injured birds. They had solved the problem of invading field mice eating the birds' food by putting a tray of scraps for the mice on the ground outside. As they explained, it saved the mice the perilous climb up the stone wall to the scullery window to be pecked for their pains.

In the narrow lanes, the banks were covered with hart's-tongue fern, but the hedgerows looked as menacing as Triffids, for the high winds had blown away all the fluff balls from the old man's beard and the tendrils blew out and made sinister clutches at passers-by.

The village of Bisley is a typical example of the steep hill villages near Stroud. The main street, lined with the well-weathered grey stone houses of former merchants, is too steep and narrow to suffer from tourist coaches. There

Miserden

are no front gardens with alpines and valerian hanging from the walls, like those which line the steep road through Bourton-on-the-Hill; the houses are flush with the pavement. Bisley should be explored on foot. Climb up the path which leads to the church, which is neary 800 feet above sea level, look across to the other steep side of the narrow valley at the stone cottages which cling desperately to the hillside and above them to the great stone barns of the farms on the hilltop. In the churchyard, there is a thirteenth-century stone well-head. It is six-sided, with blind arches, crowned by a miniature spire and cross, built, it is believed, to contain a light for the souls of the poor. It is known in the village as the 'Bonehouse', because the body of a priest was found in the well, before the present cover was put over it. In the days when the rich mill owners in the Stroud valley built houses for themselves in Bisley, they erected galleries for their families in the church, each one reached by its own private staircase from the churchyard . . . a period when folks obviously kept themselves to themselves. During the Victorian restorations, the conglomeration of stone steps on all sides of the church, together with the doors and galleries, were removed. Unlike some restored churches, it still contains many interesting items, particularly the bowl of a Norman font, which was found in a field called Church Piece, believed to have been the site of the original Norman church. The bowl is elaborately carved on the outside with large conventional designs and fleurs-de-lis, but more rare are the two fishes carved inside the basin, appearing to swim happily when it is full of holy water. Incised stone coffin lids of the eleventh century have been reset in the north wall. Beautiful carved stone cherub heads lie in casual disarray on one of the windowsills, there is no clue from whence they came. Two jolly musicians, carved in wood, obviously enjoying their fifteenth-century music, stand in a corner—possibly relics from the roof restoration. Others of their band have been placed in the roof of the vestry.

Pagan worship took place on the hills at Bisley. Two Roman altars were found built into the old church walls. A Roman statue of Mars was found on Scrubs Hill and is now in the museum at Stroud. Close to All Saints' Church is the privately owned fifteenth-century house, Overcourt,

Edgeworth. The fine Manor House, built in 1700, overlooking the wooded valley leading to Pinbury Park

which was granted to Elizabeth I before she became Queen. When King Henry VIII was wishful of forgetting Anne Boleyn, he sent her child, the young Princess Elizabeth, to stay at Overcourt. Legend has it she sickened and died and no one had the courage to inform His Majesty. Only a small boy could be found to take her place. He was red-haired, remarkably like her in face and stature and well versed in Latin. He was trained in the part he must play when Henry saw his supposed daughter again. Bisley folk are proud of their 'Bisley Boy' and will tell you why the Queen said that her heart beat like a man's, why she suffered from amenorrhoea, went bald in middle age, and dare not marry. A coffin of a female child was found at Overcourt during some alterations.

In the lane which turns off the main street round the base of the steep churchyard are Bisley Wells, restored by Thomas Keble in 1863. Five springs issue from an elegant stone semicircle while two others flow into stone cattle troughs. These are dressed with flowers once a year, by the local children in his memory. Thomas, brother of John Keble, famous for his book of sacred verse *The Christian Year*, was vicar at Bisley in 1827. He and his brother Thomas married sisters and both wedding services took place at Bisley. The Keble brothers, together with John Henry Newman (who later embraced the Catholic faith and became Cardinal Newman), were the founders of the

Bisley. The thirteenth-century Poor Souls' Light in All Saints' churchyard, thought to be the only exterior specimen in England

Oxford Movement, which revived the Anglican church services.

There is much typical Cotswold building to be seen in and around Bisley. Past the Bear Inn, originally the seventeenth-century Court House, are some new bungalows, where a forge has been set up by Norman Bucknell. He is the son of Alfred Bucknell of Sapperton, the wheelwright

Bisley. The Bear Inn

who worked for Ernest Gimson. Norman was apprenticed to his father and also to Peter Waals, but eventually from his many skills he chose to be an ornamental smith. For twenty years he worked in stable premises in Bisley, until he was compelled to move to his new bungalow. A master craftsman, he is shy and retiring and prefers "to shelter under a mushroom rather than sit on top".

Further along the road, identified by the protective iron railings erected by the Gloucestershire County Council, but almost buried beneath rampant brambles, is a headless cross date A.D. 700 and once carved with figures. It was brought from Stancombe crossroads in 1820, to serve as a Bisley boundary stone. A strange piece of economy, when the Victorians were spending so much money on the destruction and restoration of the Cotswold Norman churches.

The Bisley Commons were enclosed in 1869, causing great hardship to the families of the weavers. Their livestock were deprived of the good grazing on the land behind Chalford and the Oakridge villages. Their cattle would have ranged around the barrow called Money Tump, over what is known as Golden Coffin Field and on the site of the twenty-nine roomed Roman villa, at this time covered with grazing land. At Oakridge, the church of St Bartholomew was built for Thomas Keble in 1837. Prior to that, the most noteworthy sermon heard at Oakridge was given by the Rev. William Jenkins in 1794, when the Methodists were spreading their gospel among the Cotswold villagers. Their chapel was built in 1798 and the minister worked hard to convert his flock, preaching every weekday at 5 p.m., an unheard-of devotion to duty. A Sunday school was started by William Knee, whose life's work was devoted to trying to relieve the squalid working conditions of the weavers in the nearby Stroud valley of Randwick. They were notorious for their drunkenness, especially on the occasion of the Randwick Wap.

The beautiful Isle's Farm at Oakridge, built in 1614, was modernized in 1914 by Norman Jewson for Sir William Rothenstein, at that time Director of the Tate Gallery. The interior was decorated with Jewson's fine plaster work. In the early twentieth century, Oakridge became another centre of the arts. In a cottage at Far Oakridge, Theo. Merrett works as a bookbinder and artist in leather. He is a member of the Gloucester Guild of Craftsmen and has been responsible for most of the presentation books in Gloucestershire—one for the Queen to sign at the opening of the Severn Bridge, the Winston Churchill Memorial Book for Tetbury, many beautifully tooled bindings for church and cathedral use. One example was particularly interesting, a first folio of Shakespeare, printed for the bookseller Thomas Cotes in 1623. This had been handsomely rebound and the old paper repaired.

This book is worth thousands of pounds, since most of this edition was destroyed in the Great Fire of London. Other interesting work undertaken by him includes embossed and repoussé heraldic shields, which have to be renewed when valuable leather chairs are reupholstered. Amongst his own samples were the arms of some of the Oxford colleges, of the Dean and Chapter of Gloucester Cathedral and of the Bishop of Portsmouth.

I walked into Sapperton from Frampton Mansell on a glorious October day, when the surrounding woods were ablaze with colour and saw like Elroy Flecker the carpets of leaves lit by shafts of sunlight.

> . . . autumn leaves like blood and gold
> That strew a Gloucester lane.

I passed a row of cottages called 'The Barracks', built to house the navvies who dug the Thames and Severn Canal tunnel. This long tunnel was opened officially by George III in 1792, though with little ceremony, as the local gentry mistook the date. In the village church, a lady was arranging lavish displays of pink Nerine lilies, which grow prolifically at the foot of sheltered stone walls, often flowering well into November.

St Kenelm's is a small church, but not one to pass by. The handsome timbered roof is matched by the fine Elizabethan panelling and the carving on the front of the gallery and on the box pews. This decorative woodwork was brought from Sapperton Manor after the death of Sir Robert Atkyns in 1711. The Elizabethan manor house had previously belonged to the Poole family and the ornate marble tomb in the church is that of Sir Henry Poole (1616), his wife and family. One of his daughters-in-law stands nonchalantly, head in hand, her elbow resting on the slab—a look of utter boredom on her face. The other great tomb is that of Sir Robert Atkyns, the Gloucestershire historian, "a fair and honest judge". This virtuous man was so hostile to the intrigues at the court of Charles II, he was dismissed from the bench.

The churchyard has many well-lettered brass memorial plates dating from 1600 onwards, including some names of the Sapperton Group. Ernest Gimson (1919), architect, but better known for his well-designed furniture, the two Barnsleys, Sidney and Ernest (1926), architects and craftsmen, and Emery Walker, calligrapher and type designer. Ernest Gimson and the Barnsleys were members of the Arts and Crafts Exhibition Society, which first exhibited in 1888. Like other groups of that time, they had become acutely aware that the industrial revolution had lowered the status of craftsmen. A growing number of factories competed to flood the country with ever cheaper, shoddier and ill-designed goods. Unlike Ashbee and many

Sapperton. The village and St Kenelm's churchyard

others inspired by William Morris, the members of the Sapperton Group were not disciples of socialism. They had begun their careers with a solid architectural training—Ernest Gimson and Ernest Barnsley with J. D. Sedding, W. R. Lethaby and Sidney Barnsley with Norman Shaw, who is well known for his Queen Anne revival in architecture and his reinterpretation of classic traditions. The Sapperton Group issued no social manifesto, they dedicated themselves to purity of design and first-class workmanship.

When they left London to settle at Sapperton, they lived first at Pinbury Park, until Lord Bathurst decided he would like to restore the house for his own use. Then he made it possible for them to build or restore cottages for themselves around Sapperton. In the Middle Ages, Pinbury was a nunnery, with an avenue of yews, still called Nuns' Walk. Here, the ghost of a cheerful nun housekeeper used to be seen skipping along, bowling a large Double Gloucester cheese.

On a visit to Sapperton, I lunched with Norman Jewson, whose architectural influence spreads far and wide over the Cotswolds. His book *I Chanced to Rove* explains how, as a young man, he worked with Gimson and the Barnsleys. He was living at Bachelors' Court at Sapperton, a house he had converted from three cottages which once housed three jolly, long-lived bachelors.

We talked about Daneway House and B. J. Fletcher, who lived there for fourteen years and who had introduced me to the delightful walks in the district. His favourite walk was across to Pinbury Park, to talk with the poet John Masefield. Daneway House has been a manor since the fourteenth century and in the great hall B.J. had to remove layer after layer of paint: the white of the Victorians, which had followed the 'old oak' graining as fashions changed, until he finally revealed the beauty of the fine Elizabethan oak beams. He had personally scraped the paint from the front door with meticulous care and pride in his workmanship, in spite of the complaints from his wife, whose only refuge was by the warmth of her new Aga. He dug up a flint hatchet in the rose garden, confirming his theory that people had been living on the site since the Stone Age. Ulf the Dane had been ejected from the property by Ralph Todeni, standard-bearer to William the Conqueror. Henry de Clifford had been recorded in 1339 as living there. The Hancock family occupied the house from 1397 to 1860.

The stables were converted by the Sapperton Group into workshops. Ernest Gimson and the Barnsley brothers drew inspiration from the native English tradition of working in timber, which had developed from the days of building the great sailing ships and continued down to the making of farm carts. Gimson, not himself a working craftsman but an architect-designer, had a genius for understanding craftsmen and inspiring them to finer work.

When the group moved to Sapperton, there was a small sawmill at Daneway, at the bottom of the valley. Edward Gardiner, a son of the proprietor, joined Gimson as a chair-maker. Lord Bathurst lent Daneway House to Gimson for use as showrooms. He started furniture-making with four good London craftsmen and a Dutch foreman, Peter Waals. The workshops attracted local lads as apprentices and many of them became fine craftsmen. Peter Waals's standard of workmanship was so high that splendid pieces of furniture were created in the Daneway workshops. This was not Gimson's original intention, but there was no demand for the simple cottage furniture he wished to make and market cheaply to replace the mass-produced furniture then on sale.

At that time, there were two blacksmiths' shops in Sapperton village, employing four or five smiths. In Alfred Bucknell, son of one of the wheelwrights, Gimson found a most responsive craftsman. Before long, he was producing the intricate hinges and some of the wrought-iron gates required for the buildings which the Barnsleys and Norman Jewson were designing. Tragedy struck them all when Ernest Gimson, their leader and inspiration, died suddenly in 1919, at the age of fifty-five. Soon afterwards, the workshops had to close and all the craftsmen dispersed. Peter Waals set up at Chalford, Alfred Bucknell's son Norman carries on his father's tradition at Bisley, and Harry Gardiner joined the Gordon Russell workshops.

Norman Jewson showed me photographs of his buildings and conversions, spread out on a Sidney Barnsley table. Facing us was a Gimson dresser. The room was lit by his wall candle sconces of pierced brass, with a backing design of entwined fritillaries, flowers which grow wild around Sapperton. The sconces were made for him by Alfred Bucknell. In the hall was some of his own decorative plasterwork, a craft which he and Ernest Gimson revived to use in many of their more elaborate Cotswold houses. The example in his own hall was simple and depicted owls and squirrels, put in to please his children as was the case with the small green chair which stood under the window. At first glance it seemed an ordinary children's round-backed chair, but when examined more closely it revealed carved and painted village characters supporting the back rail: the shepherd, the blacksmith, the baker, the wheelwright and the parson, all delicately carved by Norman Jewson.

Sir Emery Walker, who lived at Daneway House after the death of Gimson, had been associated with William Morris's Kelmscott Press and was a founder of the Doves Press. The Doves Bible, in five volumes, is one of the

157

finest achievements in English book-making.

When Oliver Hill, architect to the Queen Mother, lived at Daneway, he took under his wing a struggling stone-carver, Simon Verity, allowing him to use the Gimson workshops. Verity was influenced by the fine lettering of Emery Walker and began by accepting small commissions. Since then, his work, expressing his modern ideas and dedicated craftsmanship, has spread far beyond the Cotswolds; from a simple carved bowl in Sapperton church to an important commission in Canterbury Cathedral. At his Old School House in Wiltshire, he now works in a variety of media, including stone, marble, wood and metal, but the warm responsive Cotswold stone was his first love. Norman Jewson died in 1975 and it is so appropriate that Simon Verity will engrave his tombstone.

Following the death of Oliver Hill, Daneway and the workshops were occupied by various tenants—legal and illegal. At present, the house is divided into two; in one half lives Robyn Denny, the renowned modern painter, while his brother Sir Anthony Denny, a designer, occupies the other. The Dennys are gradually restoring the house and garden. The workshops have been converted into a cottage for a husband who works as a basket-maker, his wife spinning her own wool for knitting. One surprising member of the household is Lady Denny's adopted Laotian daughter, who came out to greet me in the drive and in true oriental fashion, wished to offer me a present. She picked up a handful of Cotswold stone chippings from the drive, bowed and gracefully gave me her small gift. I bowed in return, hastily searched in the car and was able to hand her mine. She then led me by the hand into the house. I wondered what she would make of Daneway and the Cotswolds in the years to come.

The Tumps which lie between Sapperton and Tunnel House result from the waste when shafts were sunk to raise the stone from the tunnel, most of the $2\frac{1}{4}$ miles of which was cut through solid rock. Unlike public works of that period which left eyesores in their wake, the tumps from the Sapperton Tunnel were planted with trees. Tunnel House, almost in the centre of Hailey Wood, is a free house, serving excellent ale, and visitors may take the steep path down to the dried-up canal. Unfortunately, the canal was a fiasco as it leaked, though Norman Jewson said he went through the tunnel in a barge some fifty years ago. What is interesting is the tunnel entrance arch, in dressed stone, with a battlemented parapet, and empty alcoves awaiting statues. The Thames and Severn Canal, which ran from Framilode on the Severn to Inglesham at Lechlade on the Thames, was destined to failure because of the abnormal number of locks. When the Great Western Railway was opened, the company bought up the canal, stopped all traffic on it allowing it to become derelict. The Waterway Recovery Group are hoping during the next twenty years to repair the waterways from Framilode to Inglesham. Work has already started in the Sapperton Tunnel and Brian Russell of Tetbury has been commissioned to restore the classical eastern portal.

The original intention was to place two statues in the niches provided between the archway and the columns. These were to be of Father Thames and Sabrina—Sabrina being the Roman name for the River Severn. It is hoped that either funds or a willing sculptor may be found to provide figures of Father Thames and Mother Sabrina.

The Daneway Inn stands beside one of the former locks which raised the Thames and Severn Canal to the tunnel entrance. It was built for the refreshment of bargees and 'leggers' who propelled the barges through the tunnel

159

Chalford, which rises abruptly 300 to 400 feet above Golden Valley. The precipitous lanes were wide enough for the laden pack-horses which carried yarn and cloth between the homes of the weavers and the valley mills. They are unsuitable for cars

CHAPTER NINE

Chalford to Wotton-under-Edge

The Golden Valley lies between Sapperton and the Stroud valleys; a stretch of country almost Canadian in its autumn splendour, though the cottage weavers of the eighteenth century said it was so called because of the gold made by the rich from the sweated labour of the poor. The River Frome and the Thames and Severn Canal lie side by side in the valley between Stroud and Chalford, where many mills were built between 1750 and 1820— "With handsome mills this craggy dell doth teem" was written in 1824.

Twenty-two water mills were recorded in the Stroud valleys in 1086. By 1180, many had ceased to grind corn and were used for fulling or felting cloth. By 1608, half the villagers in the neighbourhood were employed in the weaving trade and this continued until the industry started to collapse in 1821. Many factors contributed to this, the stubbornness and independence of the workers, spinning and weaving in their own homes; long hours, low wages, strikes, followed by appalling poverty and the theft of cloth. Fearful for their work, they fought against the introduction of power looms in the 1820s, and ducked the Clothiers' Committee in the Stroudwater Canal. In 1839, a special Parliamentary Commission reported on the distress in the Stroud area. The market for their fine cloth went into a permanent decline and the very steepness of the terrain defied economical mechanization. New, cheap materials were manufactured in the north. Families had to leave the district and many accepted officially assisted emigration. Clothiers went bankrupt and their mills and cottages were left derelict.

On the map of 1900, only eighteen mills are shown and of these, many have been converted to private houses—conversely, some of the larger houses of the clothiers which are near to the comparatively new A419 have been converted into commercial premises. If only one could see Chalford from the air, it would look as if the buildings had been shaken out from a sack. They are scattered on the steep hillsides and lie cluttered in the valley below.

In coaching days, the road came down the steep hill from Bisley, stopped at The Company's Arms by the church and then climbed the opposite hill to Minchinhampton. The Company's Arms Inn, previously a private house named Chalford Place, recorded in the fifteenth century, is now used for light industry, but fortunately it is scheduled for preservation and has received a restoration grant. The round house occupied by the canal maintenance man has also been rescued and is used as a small canal museum. My particular interest among the remaining mills was Chestnut House and Mill, the home and workshops of Peter Waals. While the cloth industry flourished, these premises were occupied by a master weaver. The subsequently vacant mill was ideal for Waals's purpose when he had to leave the Daneway workshops at Sapperton, after the death of Ernest Gimson in 1919. The house and mill stand under the steeply rising High Street, behind a petrol station. The façade is plastered eighteenth century, with Tuscan columns and pediment, but older portions of the original sixteenth-century house are visible at the rear.

The firm now occupying the mill was making items in fibreglass and plastic. One of the young men who was operating a press proved to be knowledgeable about Peter Waals. He sent me across the road to talk to Owen Scrubey, who was working in an attic workshop approached by a rickety outside staircase. Owen had been apprenticed to Peter Waals in 1921 and was pleased to talk about the heavily built Dutchman who had come from Holland to be Gimson's first foreman. Gimson always

acknowledged his debt to Peter Waals, a fine craftsman, good designer, and perfectionist. When Waals was his own master, each piece which came from his workshop was craftsmanship at its best. A few pieces can be seen at the Cheltenham and Leicester Museums and at Arlington Mill at Bibury, but his finest work was made to order and is dispersed in the manors of the Cotswolds. It can only be seen on rare occasions, such as the Craft Festival which was held at Rodmarton Manor in 1972 to raise money for the churches at Rodmarton and Tarlton. Owen Scrubey had made the magnificent red chests in the hall at Rodmarton. Like several other pieces at the Manor, they were painted with beautiful flower designs by Alfred and Louise Powell, who for many years decorated pieces of Wedgwood china. Owen Scrubey also made the font cover in Chalford church, which was designed by Norman Jewson. It is topped by a silver dove, the work of the late George Hart of Chipping Campden.

Cotswold arts and crafts are well represented in this eighteenth-century church, restored and enlarged as the result of the untiring money-raising efforts of Thomas Keble. Noteworthy are the font by the sculptor William Simmonds, who spent much of his life in the Cotswolds, the lectern, inlaid with ivory and mother-of-pearl, by Peter Waals, panelling and sanctuary ceiling by Norman Jewson, and the four nave windows designed by Edward

Payne and made in his studio at nearby Box. The monument to Richard Thomas is by John Thomas, who became a friend of Prince Albert and whose work may also be seen at the Houses of Parliament.

Owen Scrubey talked of his fellow apprentice Sir George Trevelyan, who opened the Ernest Gimson Exhibition in Leicester in 1969. In his address, he said that after leaving Cambridge, undecided about his future career, he spent two years with Peter Waals: "For a young man of 23, it was a wholly satisfying experience; my bench, looking up the canal, was next to that of Peter Smith, the foreman. Peter Burchett was my instructor, neat, gentle and polite but absolutely firm in his demand for perfection in workmanship. My friend and contemporary was Owen Scrubey."

"We still have our excitements round here," Mr Scrubey said. "When they were filming *John Halifax, Gentleman*, they used Old Chalford Mill just behind here for the exterior shots. As you can imagine, all the village came out to watch and the bobby, he has to come fussing along on his motor bike to see what was going on—revs up his engine and spoils their period sound track."

The steep High Street of Chalford is not for motorists, it is first gear up and down with few passing places. High Street and the branching side streets were built for donkeys and if you have any horse sense, you will go on foot.

There are buildings of many periods, six chapels, clothiers' houses, weavers' cottages and storehouses—the four-storey Thanet Cottage was a storehouse. On Rack Hill, the buildings stand on man-made terraces where formerly the cloth was dried. At the extreme end is Valley Inn and a pretty walk along a reasonably level lane to Beakers Mill.

To the west is the equally steep Toadsmoor Valley, where there are still many precipitous lanes the width of a laden packhorse, leading into the village of Bussage and down to the old canal basin at Brimscombe. Thomas Keble persuaded Oxford undergraduates to raise the money for the church at Bussage, which was built in 1844. Previously, the Nonconformists, Congregationalists, Baptists and Methodists had been attending chapels at Chalford. John Wesley and the Gloucester-born preacher George Whitefield had spread the Gospel far and wide; Whitefield often preached at eventide in the open, with a record congregation in 1739 of 10,000 at Chalford. Many of the people had walked a long way after a hard day's work and had to walk home after dusk.

The Thames and Severn Canal connected with the Stroudwater Canal at Wallbridge and joined the Thames at Inglesham; 27 miles long, it was opened in 1789, but the Thames Commissioners failed to make the upper reaches of the Thames navigable. The Chalford/Inglesham section closed in 1927, the Stroud/Chalford section survived until 1933. The towpath from Wallbridge to Chalford is fair but it is rough from Chalford to the Sapperton tunnel.

Little now remains of the once busy little canal port at Brimscombe, with its large basin and wharves, where goods were transferred from the river-going vessels to the canal longboats. At one time, there was a foundry and engineering works supplying and maintaining the machinery in the mills, and also a boat-builder's yard. The buildings were demolished and the basin filled in about 1960. One reminder of its former waterway connection is the Ship Inn, with its signboard of a Severn trow, a sailing river barge. Another is a plaque on the premises occupied by International Systems Ltd, which was previously the Canal Company's Headquarters.

> It is allowed
> That Stroud
> Holds nought that's pretty,
> Wise or witty. (Anon.)

This old Cotswold jingle describes a town which has been a manufacturing centre for centuries.

Industrial depression does not foster beautiful buildings but there are some interesting walks in Stroud's older, steep streets. Most of the churches and chapels date from the early nineteenth century, with the exception of the Wesleyan Chapel in Acre Street, built in 1763.

The Subscription Rooms (1833) is a dignified building; some of the Shambles and market area is late sixteenth century—a later long arcade is of cast iron. The School of Science and Art, now a museum, is almost a mini St Pancras Hotel in the elaborate Ruskinian Gothic style.

One old industry still flourishes in Stroud: thanks to the requirements of film and television companies, Ben Ford's company will supply any horse-drawn vehicle, from a Celtic cart to an elaborate stage coach.

The construction of the new ring road has of necessity caused the demolition of many buildings. The best vantage point for an overall view of the town is the windy heights of Rodborough Common.

Just north of Stroud is the now well-known village of Slad, immortalized by Laurie Lee in his *Cider with Rosie*. There was a cloth mill at Steanbridge until 1825; the house is Elizabethan at the back, with a late eighteenth-century façade. It is depicted in one of the mural paintings at the rectory at Bishops Cleeve now assumed to be the 'Squire's House' in Laurie Lee's book. Hazel Mill, also converted, was a working cloth mill until 1870.

The walks over Rodborough Common pass a long barrow called The Toots, because of the gash in the centre dividing it into two parts. On the King Stanley side, Ivy

Lodge Barrow was largely destroyed in 1928, when a Beaker-type skeleton was unearthed, with the remains of a Roman cremation. A cattle-gridded lane leads down to Woodchester. Halfway down this hill village is a notice "No through road" and along here is the abandoned church of St Mary and Woodchester Old Priory, now private property. Up the steps set in the churchyard wall and over the stile-stone bring you into the deserted churchyard, where many of the handsome tombs have been moved, to expose only once every ten years the fine Roman mosaic pavement depicting Orpheus playing his lute and charming his beautifully drawn animal companions. It seems sad that in this expensive Space Age, money cannot be found to preserve and find adequate cover for the mosaics, as has been done so well at Fishbourne Palace at Chichester.

To allow the design to be on view under ideal conditions at all times, an exact replica is being made by the mosaic workers of the Abbey Studios, Wotton-under-Edge under the direction of Mr Howard Woodward. The replica is being laid on the floor of the Rowland Hill Tabernacle at Wotton and will be viewed from a gallery. His modern mosaic workers are faithfully copying the work of the Romans to the best of their highly skilled ability. The Woodchester tesserae are ceramic, in six colours. The Romans obtained the light and dark reds from a form of brick-like tile; the lighter tan from sandstone and the off-white from the local limestone. The grey-blue was produced by baking the local lias clay. These colours together with the dark grey-blue were all obtained within a fifty-mile radius of Woodchester. They are being reproduced from the materials used by the Romans, baking the lias clay in 12-inch lengths of $\frac{1}{2}$-inch width, allowing them to form their own natural twists, so that when cut into $\frac{1}{2}$-inch tesserae, they have the same uneven stone-like texture of the original Roman ones. Considering that 42 per cent of the original Orpheus pavement has been destroyed, the reproduction with the missing sections also reproduced will be even more exciting, and to quote several leading authorities in the archaeological world, "one will soon be able to visit Wotton-under-Edge and see the complete masterpiece, as the Romans would have viewed it on completion 1,600 years ago". As thousands of people saw the original pavement in 1973 under almost impossibly cramped conditions, it is to be hoped this new venture will meet with the success it deserves.

Making an exact reproduction of the Orpheus pavement is slow work but it is hoped to have it on view to the public at the tabernacle at Wotton-under-Edge in the near future.

Minchinhampton Common is an area covering nearly 600 acres and rising to 600 feet above sea level. It was given

165

to the town by a nun, Dame Alice Hampton, daughter of John Hampton, whose tomb is in the church. The common is now preserved by the National Trust. Local children can play their mock battles around the Iron Age earthworks, over the massive rampart and ditch known as the Bulwarks. This extends to Woeful Dames Bottom; here is was that the Danes were defeated in battle. It is not clear whose dames were woeful. Two standing stones by the ditch are aptly named Hengist and Horsa. Six roads meet on the highest part of the common at Tom Long's Post, a notorious haunt of highwaymen until Tom Long was caught. Then it was "the post upon the common, where they be hanging poor Tom Long".

The long barrow is called Whitefield's Tump, in memory of the reformer George Whitefield, who preached there in 1745 to 1,200 people. A year later, the Methodist preacher Mr Adams was not so well received, being first ducked in a tanner's pit and then thrown into Bourne Brook.

Minchinhampton, a version of Hampton to which was prefixed Monachyn (the village of the nuns), developed with the growth of the wool trade and in the twelfth century the flocks belonging to the nuns alone numbered 2,000. In F. W. Harvey's words,

The sheep our wold doth breed
Scorn not, for they do feed
And clothe a man in need.

By 1724, the village had developed into one of the important centres which marketed the cloth made by the mills in the valleys below. Buying and selling was first conducted in the Market House, built in 1698, but trade overflowed into the wide High Street, the eighteenth-century Crown Hotel, and the other crowded hostelries. It is hard to visualize this teeming scene in the quiet square of today.

For those who like the delicious flavour of cabbage bread (a loaf baked in cabbage leaves), the baker in Minchinhampton will oblige. Apart from the High Street or Square, the other streets are narrow and lined with compact stone houses—no place to meet three farm boys trying to round up six playful bullocks; fortunately it was early on a Sunday morning and the streets were deserted.

The church of Holy Trinity at Minchinhampton, together with the sister church at Avening, was given by William I to the Abbaye aux Dames at Caen and both churches remained under their jurisdiction until the suppression of all alien houses in the reign of Henry V. Some of the Norman and fourteenth-century building remains, including the fourteenth-century effigies of Sir Peter de la

Minchinhampton, a large village on a high plateau

Mere and his wife, believed to have been the donors of the transept. There are several early brasses to wealthy clothiers and a regrettably small brass plate records the death of James Bradley in 1762. This man, who was born at nearby Sherborne in 1693, became a Fellow of the Royal Society, Savillian Professor of Astronomy at Oxford, and Astronomer Royal. It was his accurate observations at Greenwich which laid the foundation for modern observational astronomy and has led us to the Space Age, yet his home town makes little boast of its great man.

In the churchyard, many ornamental shrubs surround the baroque tombstones; on the first day of spring, pink and white daphne, forsythia, prunus, early berberis and dogwood were providing a riot of colour above the daffodils and beds of large pink saxifrage.

Box House, partly seventeenth century, was once a Pest House, housing plague victims. Later, it was occupied by Drs Haywood and Browne when an epidemic of smallpox raged through the Cotswold villages in 1768. These two doctors developed a primitive method of inoculation, an arm-to-arm transfer from a mildly infected patient. Their difficulty, not surprisingly, was to persuade the terrified patients to try it.

The market was built by Phillip Sheppard about 1700. He bought the Manors of Minchinhampton and Avening in 1651 to establish a wool market. The building was

given to the town in 1913 by Henry Ricardo, who transferred his manorial rights to the National Trust in 1944. It is now used by the local dramatic society.

At the north-east end of the village is the seventeenth-century Blue Boys Farmhouse, which was the old coaching inn. The original inn sign of two dyers (known as blue-boys), with their vat, is in the Museum at Stroud. On the south side of the village is the sunny terraced hillside of the old vineyards and the site of de-la-Mere's Manor, now occupied by Lammas House.

I was on the common one morning to watch the sunrise, and saw the grass, described by Mary Bewley—

> Mornings enchanted in a silver haze
> Of dew and cobweb, fading into air
> Sunwarmed at last.

It was as if millions of spiders had moved in overnight and decorated the grass with crystal chandeliers. I have seen an army of rats on the move but I have yet to see an army of marching spiders!

Many of the walks over the common lead down to the surrounding villages. At Amberley, in Rose Cottage, Mrs Craik wrote *John Halifax, Gentleman*. The cottage bears no plaque but is a double-fronted house on the corner of the lane leading down to Pinfarthing. In the valley below is

Amberley. A woodland lane which clearly shows the difference in terrain from that of the wold country

Dunkirk Mill, which plays an important part in her story. It is no longer a working mill; the premises have been divided for use by small industries. The buildings date from 1789–1855. In its heyday, it was powered by five waterwheels and a beam engine.

The small village of Box, which clings to the steep side of the common, is distinguished by the gilded spirelet of the small church of St Barnabas. The east and west windows are by Edward Payne and those by his father, Henry

The small village of Avening

Payne, may be seen in the Roman Catholic chapel. Henry Payne, an established Birmingham stained-glass artist, moved his studio to Box in the 1920s, to be near his father-in-law, Charles Gere, a well-known artist living in Cheltenham. Henry was a friend of Sidney Barnsley at Sapperton and of Alfred and Louise Powell, the decorative painters, at Rodmarton. Because of Henry's enthusiasm, Box soon became a centre for the arts. Exhibitions were held regularly at the seventeenth-century St Loe's House at Amberley, until the formation of the Gloucester Guild, now exhibiting annually at Painswick and Chipping Campden.

It is rare for a town dweller to be welcomed into a country house with the greeting "It is wonderful to have a breath of Birmingham!", but such was mine, at the studio of Edward Payne. Admittedly we had been at the Birmingham School of Art together and had many mutual friends. Edward's beautiful windows are in churches all over the Cotswolds, but his favourite design is at the fifteenth-century church of St George at Didbrook, near Hailes. It depicts ordinary people rather than biblical characters, and their journey up the tree of life. Few laymen realize the amount of art work, the hundreds of detailed drawings of drapery, portraits, illustrations of fauna and flora, which have to be completed before any craftwork with glass and metal can begin.

So much is being done in the Cotswolds at the moment to prevent the influx of townees and their purchasing of second homes, Edward Payne thinks the local county councils would do well to remember the amount of derelict village property which was rescued between the wars by industrialists from the Midlands. There is one such in Box, whose wealth spreads like a warm glow over all the village activities.

Stone for the Houses of Parliament was quarried at Balls Green. The old stone mines were closed in 1940 but 2,000 yards of passages have been preserved and may be visited with a guide. If you walk down the field path from Balls Green past Longford Farm, you pass Gatcombe Water, with its great variety of wildfowl. This 15-acre pond was dug in 1806 to enable Longford Mill to continue working. At this mill, the Playne family are still weaving cloth for the world's tennis balls. In his *History of the Parishes of Minchinhampton and Avening* (1915) Arthur Twisden Playne, describing the valleys, says: "Avening is situated in one of the most beautiful"—but that was in 1915. Today, the valley road through the village keeps its old character, but modern housing estates have been allowed to litter the hillsides. The village stands high above the River Avon from which it takes its name.

In the small but excellent church museum, there is a model of the ancient tombs unearthed in a field called the Norn, above the hamlet of Nagshead, and from this evidence it is thought that Avening was inhabited as early as 3000 B.C. The stone coffin beside the porch and the skeleton of a girl in the museum with skeletons of birds at her feet suggest a pre-Conquest burial ground, and local farmers at various times have found many coins and pieces of pottery from the Roman occupation. There may have been a Saxon church on the site before the Norman one, dedicated in 1080. Three models in the museum show clearly the development of the building, from the simple Norman church, through the Early English, Decorated, Perpendicular and modern periods. After first inspecting the models, it is interesting to trace the alterations within the existing building. In the church is the tomb of Henry Brydges (1615), the fourth son of Lord Chandos of Sudeley, a wild young man, freebooter and notorious pirate, until he married the daughter of Samuel Sheppard, a wealthy clothier, who had purchased the Manor of Avening. Brydges then settled at Avening Court, under the watchful eye of his father-in-law; the present house has been considerably altered since his time. The Court, like the church, is on an ancient site and a view of both the park and the house can be enjoyed from the lane which leads along the ridge above to the hamlet of Nagshead. In pre-Conquest days, the estate belonged to Brittric, Lord of Gloucester, who bred his hunting hawks there, and I saw in the surrounding country several possible descendants of Brittric's hawks; the country folk call them windhovers, their hovering described by Gerard Manley Hopkins: "... high there, how he rung upon the rein of a wimpling wind". I had the good fortune to see a much rarer member of the falcon family, a merlin, in the country between Avening and Cherington.

In 1788, Dr Edward Jenner of Berkeley purchased the Chantry at Avening to begin his married life and to develop his lifelong study of vaccination as a preventative treatment. His research has proved a great gift to mankind. His hobby was bird watching; he it was who solved the mystery of the infant cuckoo and how, once hatched, the young bird manages to clear the foster parents' nest of their own eggs and young. Jenner died in 1823 and is buried in the family vault at Berkeley.

In the old village Police House, John Millnan, a craftsman in wood, has his business and a collection of rare wood-working tools. A small museum over his garage houses many interesting items and is open on Sundays.

Beside the lane which climbs the steep hill to Gatcombe Park are two ancient stones—The Tingle Stone, in a clump of trees on the left, which if good fortune smiled, would give a tingling in the fingers of those who touched it. Higher up, on the right, standing in a field quite near the road, is the Long Stone. This looks pock-marked, weather-beaten and far too old now to comply with the legend of its walk on Midsummer Eve. Centuries of weathering have enlarged the holes through which superstitious mothers at one time used to pass their babies to prevent them having rickets. If the baby was so small that it could be passed through the smaller hole, it was thought to have no hope of life and was liable to be destroyed, like the runt of a litter. Finally a village doctor managed to quash the superstition with a child of his own, who grew to be a fine young man.

Gatcombe Park, which lies on the opposite side of the road from the Long Stone, was built in 1770 for Edward Sheppard, a descendant of Samuel. The manor was later acquired in 1814 by David Ricardo, the celebrated political economist. His father made a fortune on the Stock Exchange, much of which his son David spent on the manor, and on the building of the churches at Amberley and Brimscombe. There are several memorial tablets to the Ricardos in Holy Trinity Church in Minchinhampton. It is good to know that Her Majesty the Queen has purchased Gatcombe Park, which has stood empty for so long. It is to be hoped that the restoration of this fine old house will bring work to the many first-class craftsmen still living in the Cotswolds.

The roads are steep in and out of Nailsworth. On one

hillside known as the Nailsworth Ladder, the road is a series of treacherous horseshoe bends, used for motorcycle rallies. All the roads lead into the centre of the town with its recent clock tower and modern shops. The more interesting streets radiate out into the surrounding hills. As in other Stroud villages, there are three different denominational chapels but two nineteenth-century churches and, on Chestnut Hill, a Quaker Meeting House. This was built in 1689, an elegant yet simple building still retaining the original seating. Spring Hill is dotted with the houses of successful clothiers of the past, and what mills remain are converted to other uses.

It was at Nailsworth that the 'Super Tramp' W. H. Davies finally settled down to write, after years of being a rolling stone. Meeting with Klondyke gold seekers, losing a leg by falling beneath a truck, travelling steerage and being desperately poor were all useful experience for his writing. He acquired a house in Nailsworth, in the Cotswold country where he loved to walk. As his books became well known, his portrait was painted by Sir William Rothenstein and his head was modelled by Jacob Epstein. His lines—

> What is this life, if full of care
> We have no time to stand and stare!

are said to have been more often quoted than lines from Shakespeare.

The road out of Nailsworth to Horsley follows the brook which is fed from a gushing spring in Kingscote Wood. By the Turnpike Tollhouse, a path drops down to the old mill. This was converted in 1882 to become the headquarters of a trout farm. It has not been enlarged since 1939, for the graded fish pools fill the entire valley bottom, fed by the excellent supply of fresh spring water from Horsley Brook. The mill house basement, at the level of the mill wheel, is filled with shallow tanks where, from December to April, the eggs are hatched and the young fish carefully nourished. The fisheries used to breed some of the famous Redmyre carp, believed to be the largest of the species in the world. Now they concentrate on brown and rainbow trout, export incubated eggs to Africa and Asia, and supply fish for restocking rivers. The fishery delivers trout in its own oxygenated tank vehicles to anywhere in Great Britain. By means of plane deliveries they are able to help fish farming in many undeveloped countries. Here, by this tributary of the River Frome, is one old mill which has continued to serve a useful purpose since the weavers left.

Above the mill, the road remains reasonably level but the village rises high above it and extends down to the valley below. After the Conquest, the manor was given to

173

the Abbey of St Martin of Trouarn in Normandy and passed in 1260 to the canons of Bruton in Somerset. St Martin's Church, like that of St Bartholomew at Nympsfield, is left with only a tower. By the west doorway there is a 'twelve o'clock' stone, on which falls the shadow of the tower at noon. An oil painting in the vestry shows the old church and the prison house which stood on the site of a priory immediately south of the church. In the basement of the present house named The Priory are traces of the prison walls. The prison was a model House of Correction, built by direction of Sir George Onesiphorus Paul; in its time, it housed the Stroud weavers who rioted in 1825 and the agricultural labourers who took part in the Swing Riots of 1830, caused by the introduction of threshing machinery.

The county historian Thomas Dudley Fosbrooke lived at the vicarage on Rockness Hill when he was vicar of St Martin's (1794–1811).

At Downend, there is a pleasant group of old houses around the White Hart Inn, but, as in many of the Stroud valleys, there is a haphazard rash of new houses on the hillsides.

I diverted from the A4058 road to explore the beautiful country on the west side, taking the lane to Nympsfield. This quiet village is only disturbed now by the noise of planes towing the gliders from the popular gliding field high above the Severn valley. It was once one of the rowdiest villages in the Stroud valleys, when in the eighteenth century magistrates had to suppress the Nympsfield Revels—a time when the drunken weavers were prepared to take on and fight all comers.

The fifteenth-century tower of St Bartholomew's with its battlements and gargoyles dominates the village, but the tower is all that exists of the original building; the remainder was rebuilt in 1861. The Rose and Crown is an interesting seventeenth-century village pub and it was here a fearful vicar of Coberley is reputed to have hidden, when Charles I was staying with the Whittingtons. The young vicar was discovered by the Roundhead soldiers, and turned out of his hiding place naked but unharmed. A friendly housemaid, to his great embarrassment, is said to have tied her long white petticoat round his neck. It looked remarkably like a surplice and he was able to make the long walk back to his parish.

It is not easy to enter Hetty Pegler's Tump, though the key may be obtained from a cottage in the village. The door is painfully small and I found it impossible even to crawl in through the wet mud. Fortunately two slender young students in patched jeans cheerfully wriggled in, used my torch and reported their findings. It is a long barrow with two side chambers. When excavated in 1854, fifteen skeletons were found. The locals will tell you that

Hetty Pegler was a witch who lived in the barrow in the Middle Ages, but Henry and Hester Pegler were in fact a respectable couple who in 1677 bought the farming land on which the barrow stands. Hetty probably liked to sit on the Tump on a summer evening and enjoy the view of the horseshoe bend of the River Severn, with the hills of Wales beyond.

Uleybury, which is lower down the hill, nearer the village, is one of the largest Iron Age hill-forts in Gloucestershire, enclosing about 32 acres. Much of the inner rampart has been destroyed by years of ploughing also, on the north side, by quarrying, but a walk remains between the ramparts.

Along the curving street at Uley towards The Green are some of the seventeenth-century period houses, reminders of the wealthy clothiers of the past. The trade of this busy market centre finally collapsed after Edward Shepperd had spent £50,000 on improvements to his mill in 1834. Three years later, costly strikes and the stubborn attitude of the weavers forced him into bankruptcy. It is hard to visualize this quiet village with one thousand people out of work, wondering how to feed their families and where else to go to find work. Apart from a firm of builders, a garage and the village shops, work for most is found in neighbouring towns and farms, though two enterprising men have occupied the long-deserted chapels.

At the top of Fop Street stands the Gothick Union Chapel, built in 1790, when the weavers founded a religion based on co-operation and brotherhood. This building has now been cleared of everything but the gallery and the organ and provides a large, light showroom for cottage antiques. The vestry at the back has become a well-equipped workshop for the renovation of all kinds of

Uley, a favourite centre for archaeologists and witch-hunters

furniture; there is no lack of work. On sale was a small book—*Secrets of the Uley Cook*. In this, some eighty local contributors have given their best recipes, and the book is illustrated by another chapel owner. The proceeds go towards the renovation of the village hall.

The Bethesda Baptist Chapel was built at the beginning of the nineteenth century, lower down the hillside in South Street, well away from the Unionists. Derelict for fifteen years, Andrew Wood repaired the schoolroom at the back for his living quarters and uses the main chapel for his ceramic sculpture. A trained artist, potter, lecturer and stonemason, he learned the Cotswold craft of stone roofing and walling. He has saved many of the local cottage roofs from being re-roofed with artificial stone. Apart from establishing his own business, his skills are generously available in the fight to preserve the Cotswold heritage.

The lane to Owlpen leaves Uley at the Green and almost at the foot of the steep hill is an unmarked track leading to the church of The Holy Cross, rebuilt in 1828. The glass mosaic wall pictures by James Powell are typical of the period, but the plaster ceiling of the nave, also painted by Powell, is almost obscured by the dark-brown, heavy wooden ribs supporting the roof.

Owlpen Manor is a unique group of buildings, consisting of the Manor and Court House, the barn, the church and the mill. They are neatly enclosed by drystone walls, with the beautiful wooded hillsides rising around them and the Ewelme stream flowing from the mill to the valley below. The church is always open, but the rest of the buildings are available to the public on one day each week during the season.

A community, probably attracted by the plentiful supply of good drinking water from the many springs which flow into the Ewelme stream, has existed on the site since Saxon times and the settlement was recorded in the Domesday survey. In the early twelfth century, Sir Bartholomew de Olepenne possessed 800 acres of land under the feudal overlordship of the Berkeleys. The last male Olepenne died in 1462 and his granddaughter Margery married John Daunte, a wealthy merchant of Wotton. It was Thomas Daunte the fourth who restored the house in the 1700s and laid out the terraced gardens, with their steps, gates and yew trees. When the last of the Dauntes married a Stoughton and built a Victorian house higher up the hill, their guests were still entertained to picnics on the lawns at Owlpen.

In 1925, Norman Jewson, collaborator with the Sapperton Group in the revival of Cotswold architecture and craftsmanship, bought the estate and painstakingly set about its restoration. When completed to his meticulous but expensive satisfaction, he could not afford to live in it

Owlpen

Wotton-under-Edge, a town of two levels

and had to sell. Later owners received a grant, recommended by the Historic Buildings Council, so that this unique group of Cotswold buildings may be preserved for the future.

The A4058 road remains fairly level until it reaches the horseshoe bends at Combe hill, and descends into Wotton-under-Edge, the last of the wool towns on my route. This was one of the Berkeley strongholds until it was destroyed by fire, when King John's mercenaries devastated the Berkeley lands. At St Mary's in Wotton are two of the finest large brasses in the Cotswolds—those of Thomas Berkeley (1417) and his wife Margaret (1392). Lord Berkeley was an admiral and is shown wearing a rare mermaid collar. The mermaid was one of the badges used by the Berkeleys. The church is full of surprises. The organ was presented originally by King George I to St Martin-in-the-Fields in 1726 and was played by Handel. It cost £1,500, but in 1799 it was acquired by the vicar of St Mary's, for £200. The handsome brass chandeliers were made in London in 1763 and the stained glass is a copy of figures by Sir Joshua Reynolds. Among the many fine memorials in the church is one to David Taylor (1833) by E. H. Bailey, whom few people remember as the designer of Nelson's Column in Trafalgar Square. Not so surprising is the fact that the later altar, the reredos and the communion rails are the work of the more local Sapperton Group.

The Berkeleys lived at Wotton at times when they were excluded from Berkeley Castle. The seventeenth-century manor house beside the church is on the site of the old Berkeley home. Lady Katherine Berkeley, who founded the grammar school in 1384, was the widow of the famous Thomas, accused of complicity in the slow, revolting, murder of Edward II at Berkeley Castle.

Some of the town's clothiers, including Jonathan Witchell, the Austins and the Adeys, are buried in the churchyard. When their industry declined, Witchell lived in near poverty, as his considerable capital was tied up in his wool business. Humphrey Austin installed the first steam-driven power looms in Gloucestershire, at his New Mills, which he built between 1806 and 1811, but strikes and the declining demand for good cloth forced the family into bankruptcy. The Adeys lived at the house on the rise of Adey's Lane, visited by Aubrey Beardsley when it was occupied by Moore Adey, a friend of Oscar Wilde.

Many other fine eighteenth-century houses of the clothiers grace the hilly streets of Wotton—Miss Ann Bear-Packer's almshouse (1837); No. 4 Old Town, a café with an interesting panelled room; Edbrook House; No. 9 Old Town, the Court House, originally a hall on the site of an earlier building, where the court of the Manor of Wotton was held; and Lloyd's Bank, formerly the Vine Inn, from which the coaches left for Cirencester. Isaac

179

Pitman first taught his stenographic shorthand while he was a master at the British School, now demolished for road widening.

When I was last wandering round the churchyard, two elderly vergers were busy with sticks, beating the church's large door mats, which were laid out upside down on the flat-topped tombs. They cheerfully stopped work to talk, the burning question that day being a refusal by the authorities to allow the local council to create more car parks.

"Wotton's a fine old town, but with all them double yellow lines, visitors can only stop at top or bottom, which makes for mighty steep walking."

We talked of the clothiers and weavers who had lived in the town and of their fine tombs—"Come in handy they do, for this job—takes all the backache out of the work when you can beat at this level."

I was sure the weavers lying beneath would have sympathized with them.

Round the back of the churchyard is an alleyway aptly named The Cloud—in bad weather it might well be above the clouds in the valley below. On a fine day, it is a good vantage point from which to look down on what was the unplanned early town behind the church and manor, with narrow passages between the cottages, leading down to the stream which eventually powered the mills—Britannia and Waterloo. One or two stone buildings can still be seen amongst those of the new housing estate covering the steep hillside. Specialized weaving continued for a time lower down the valley at Kingswood, but these mills are now to be converted into a large printing works.

In the street outside the church is the old Bluecoat School (1715), distinguished by an elegant shell hood over the door. Along Church Street are Hugh Perry's almshouses—he was a Wotton man who became Sheriff of London in 1632, his endowment provided an attractive six-gable building, and visitors are invited to walk through the arch to the small chapel. This stands in a square garden, surrounded by the almshouses, with their exterior staircases and balconies. On the opposite side is Dawes Hospital, built in 1720. Church Street joins High Street, with its haphazard shop fronts inserted below eighteenth-century façades. The Tolsey, on the corner of Market Street, boasts an elaborate bracket clock and a cupola with a copper dragon weather-vane. The National Provincial Bank demonstrates how the High Street buildings might have looked if there had been earlier planning control. The Rowland Hill's Tabernacle, with its tall grey turret, stands high on the hill by Bear Lane, towering over the town.

North Nibley. The Tyndale Monument, erected in 1866 to the memory of William Tyndale, translator of the English Bible

Ozleworth Bottom

CHAPTER TEN

The Bottoms to the Eastleaches

Every top has a bottom and the Cotswolds are no exception. After leaving Cleeve and Birdlip, the high hills, with the exception of Haresfield and Painswick Beacons, slope gently towards the plains north of Bath, in a series of deep, wooded valleys. These were formed millions of years ago by the small springs and surface water plunging down the steep incline towards the Bristol Channel. The Bristol Avon and the Frome, with all their tributaries, cut deep into the limestone and lias clay and eventually created the steep-sided, beech-covered Stroud valleys and The Bottoms.

This delightful wooded country ends at Alderley, with three long valleys incised into the hills. Tyley Bottom, with its small stream widening to a lake above the hamlet of Coombe, is a walker's paradise. The Cotswold Way goes past Coombe on the way to Bath. Walkers wishing to explore Tyley have to follow the tracks which lead up Wimley Hill to the head of the coombe, or, as they say locally, to "the top of the Bottom".

Ozleworth Bottom is a motorist's nightmare, for there are two steep, tortuous lanes leading into it. One goes from Bagpath down Brock Hill, the other along the side of Ozleworth Park. The latter is the one to take to find the rare old church at Ozleworth, which stands beyond the farm at the entrance to the Park.

This wooded valley was chosen as an ideal site by the builders of three great houses. Newark Park was reputed to have been built from the stones of Kingswood Abbey, which was demolished in 1540. Newark was given to the National Trust in 1950 by Mrs C. A. Power Clutterbuck, but of the 643 acres of wooded and agricultural land, only the footpath between the park lodges is available as yet to the public. Ozleworth Park is an eighteenth-century building, and Boxwell Court, almost at the "top of the Bottom", is where Captain Martin Huntley entertained Prince Rupert and where Charles II rested on his flight from Boscobel to Bristol. The name Boxwell comes from an ancient holy well and the magnificent box woods which cover the side of the coombe. The small thirteenth-century church of St Mary is remarkable for its massive stone bellcote, but the romance of the valley centres round St Nicolas's Church at Ozleworth. Many legends point to the circular dry-walled churchyard as belonging to a Druid or pre-Christian site. The advowson of the church was given by Roger Berkeley, who died in 1131, to the Augustinian community at Leonard Stanley. The rare central, irregular hexagonal tower dates from the time of Roger Berkeley and no doubt served as a look-out for defence purposes. The coombe was a haunt of highwaymen, and the last Englishman to be hanged for highway robbery is buried in the churchyard.

After the Cotswold Way leaves Ozleworth Bottom and Wortley it passes through Alderley, the most south-westerly corner of my choice of Cotswold country. Beyond Alderley, the landscape begins to change and the woods give way to large, undivided agricultural areas. St Kenelm's at Alderley was rebuilt in 1802, except for the fifteenth-century tower, which has a grotesque array of corbels and carved bosses. In the churchyard is the head-stone to Marianne North, a pioneer botanist who trav-elled to the far corners of the world in the nineteenth century, collecting and painting rare flora. For sixteen years she travelled alone in Canada, the West Indies and Brazil, enduring the most primitive conditions. In Japan, she nearly died of cold from working in a pretty room made of paper, with only a pan of charcoal for warmth. Even after an attack of rheumatic fever she was undefeated and left for the warmer climate of Sarawak and Java. She spent a year in England, labelling and indexing her collection of meticulous paintings in preparation for their hanging in the North Gallery at Kew Gardens, which was opened in 1882. When she found the flora of the African continent was not represented, she set off again to roam about South Africa for a year. After subsequently visiting the Sey-chelles and Chile, her health finally broke down and she was compelled to return to England in 1884. There were no honours which could be awarded to ladies in Victoria's day, but Marianne's contribution to botany was honoured by a letter from the Queen, written by Sir Henry Pon-sonby and enclosing a signed photograph of Her Majesty. Marianne spent the last five years of her life creating a garden of her own at The Mount in Alderley and in writ-ing *Recollections of a Happy Life*. A friend of her father, Sir Joseph Hooker, lived for a time at Alderley and was a fre-quent visitor to The Grange, when it was the home of the eminent oriental botanist Brian Houghton Hodgson who introduced the Himalayan rhododendron *hodgsonii* to this country.

Sir Joseph ensured that Marianne's name should also be remembered by horticulturalists. The names of the four new species she added to the botanical lists, the Nepenthes, Crinium, Areca and Kniphofia, are named *northiana*.

At Hillsley, the country changes to the flat agricultural plain, and I wandered back through the last of the beauti-fully wooded bottoms, Hennel and Bartley.

The Cotswold Way is well over to the left but there are

Waterley Bottom is for walkers. Take the path from Whiteway all along the valley to the junction which meets the lane to North Nibley—or take the path on the left, which continues between the woods towards Wooton-under-Edge

several footpaths and one passable lane which goes from Hillsley between Splatts, Sticksley and Midger Woods. This is a wonderful area for wild flowers and birds all through the season. In addition to the common birds there are blackcaps, tree-creepers, wrens and warblers. Underfoot, well nourished by leaf mould, are lords and ladies, hedge parsley, speedwell and an occasional spotted orchid, wood spanicle and tway-blade. Loath to leave this hazy paradise, I made my way north past Nan Tow's Tump. This is one of the largest round barrows in the Cotswolds, nearly 100 feet in diameter. It dates from the Bronze Age but legend does not relate when Nan Tow, the local witch, was buried there, standing upright.

Beverstone Castle, built about 1225, is a ruin on one side, and on the other the fourteenth-century domestic accommodation has been added to over the centuries. In the courtyard of the house some of the buildings are the offices for the acres of agricultural land which lie between Beverstone and the Elizabethan manor of Chavenage. Neither estate is open to the public but the pathway to St Mary's Church at Beverstone passes above the moat on the side of the ruins, which may also be seen from the churchyard.

The only Saxon relic is a mutilated pre-Conquest sculpture of the Resurrection on the south face of the church tower, although it is recorded that Beverstone was occupied by Earl Godwin in 1051, before the castle was built. In the Berkeley chapel are four thirteenth-century stone coffin covers and a brass to Elizabeth Brydges, dated 1693. They all rest at peace, but the spooky castle ruins, kept gloomy and dark by the tall trees, resounded with the squawking of a flock of jackdaws.

Cherington is a pleasant little village with its stone buildings clustered round the green. At Lowesmore Farm,

Rodmarton. The church of St Peter

beside the lane to Rodmarton, is the magnificent Lowesmore Barn—162 feet long with seventeen bays and a square tower with a columbarium. At Rodmarton is Frank Baldwin's forge where Frank and his father carried out many designs for Sidney and Ernest Barnsley after the Sapperton Group disbanded. Rodmarton Manor was the last great Cotswold manor to be built in true Cotswold style, for the Hon. Claud Biddulph. It was designed by Ernest Barnsley, who took twenty years to complete it, searching for suitable stone and matured timber to suit all his meticulous requirements. During this time, Peter Waals had moved to Chalford and set up his own workshops and he was responsible for most of the woodwork and the furniture. In the local forge at Rodmarton, Ernest Barnsley found a smith even more receptive to his ideas than Alfred Bucknell had been to Ernest Gimson's, so Frederick and young Frank Baldwin made most of the metalwork for the Manor. About ten in the morning I walked into the forge yard—what Frank Baldwin would call midday. There was no one about but a local farmer struggling to rope some repaired machinery on to his Land-Rover. In the forge was a magnificent pair of wrought-iron gates leaning against the wall, complete except for the locks and the handles, which were lying on the anvil.

"How do," said Frank, bustling in. "I can spend a bit of time with you, if you'll help me sort some bolts first." In his stockroom we rummaged through boxes of bolts and nuts to find some to tide over a farmer in distress until he could spare his machinery for a proper repair. Then Frank and I sat by the forge fire to talk about the Barnsleys.

"They were perfectionists until the day they died," he said affectionately. "Sidney came in to tell us of Ernest's death and brought with him designs for all the elaborate fittings he wanted for Ernest's coffin. I was only a lad but I remember it was the first time I worked all through the night alongside of my dad, to get them finished in time for the funeral. Sidney died soon afterwards, so Dad thought it would be a fitting tribute for us to make a similar set for Sidney and that's what we did."

I asked Frank Baldwin who had designed the magnificent pair of gates leaning against his forge wall.

"Well—a lot of me and a bit of an Italian chap called Zanni, dead now. Dad always kept all the designs he was given to work from, so they come in handy with a bit of ingenious alteration. They're for the Manor—I suppose you've been round the house?"

I said how much I had admired all the metalwork there and particularly the fender in the dining-room.

"Me too—that was the first bit of brass piercing I was entrusted to do and mighty proud of it I was. It's difficult these days to find time for fine craft work. All I seem to do

187

is run a repair shop for the local farmers. These new-fangled machines are a lot more trouble than a pair of good horses."

Time to go when yet another farmer arrived in need of Frank's urgent assistance.

For brass-rubbing enthusiasts, the restored church at Rodmarton contains a rare brass of a lawyer in cap and gown (1461). Rodmarton was the home of the Lysons family. Daniel, whose tomb (1834) is in the church, is remembered for his book on the environs of London, and his brother Samuel for his drawings of Roman antiquities discovered in England and for his excavations at Wood-chester and other Roman villas in the Cotswolds. The two brothers were editors of *Magna Britannia*, which appeared alphabetically in counties and set out to describe every town and village. Started in 1806, it was unfinished when publication had to cease in 1822, as Samuel had died in 1819. The first Samuel Lysons came to Rodmarton as rector in 1756 and the living was in the family for 137 years.

At nearby Kemble, the weathercock on the tall spire looks, in the daytime, as if he had laid two gigantic eggs. At night, these are aircraft warning lights for Kemble aerodrome. Some of the church is thirteenth century, including the tower at the base of the spire, which was added in 1824. The effigy of an unknown knight, carved in Purbeck marble (*c.* 1290), certainly looks his age.

I passed through South Cerney, an old village, recently rapidly developed to accommodate aircraft workers. Silver Street is the main street and together with Church Lane still retains some eighteenth-century houses. The gardens of the houses in Church Lane go down to one arm of the River Churn where a pleasant walk called Bow-Wow is raised up between two loops of the river. New trees have been planted by various local societies on both sides of the river, and in time these may mask the rather ugly new housing estates.

At the north end of Silver Street, known locally as the 'Upper Up', is the Tudor-Gothic Edwards College, founded by the will of Anne Edwards in 1834 as a home for the widows of clergy.

The large church was restored and altered in 1862 when the elaborate Norman doorway was moved to its present position during the alterations. It is a magnificent example of roll mouldings, beakheads, flower heads and large beast-head stops. The sculptured figure of Christ in Glory and The Harrowing of Hell are dated approximately 1135. The treasures of the church are two carefully restored wood carvings, considered to be the oldest in England. They were found in a cavity in the wall of the Norman tower in 1915. There is the head and foot of a figure of Christ, thought to have been part of a twelfth-century rood. The wood had remained intact, due to a coating of gesso, a mixture made from plaster of Paris and used as a painting surface. A leaflet available in the church compares these remains with photographs of similar carvings which have been preserved in Spain and Italy. The South Cerney carvings are small, the head barely six inches high, dated between 1125–50, and are carefully preserved with a backing of glue and sawdust.

With the increase in population, an American air base, the Concorde test runway nearby and eight large firms extracting gravel in the vicinity, the people in the new housing estates were in need of some recreational facilities. Modern small boats are readily available, water sports are becoming popular and here was the ideal site for 'The Cotswold Water Park'. Gravel has been taken from the area since 1920 and with modern mechanical devices, this has been speeded up considerably during the last twenty years. The gravel deposits are on the Oxford clay bed and drainage water collects in the pits, rising to a water table near ground surface. These lakes immediately attracted a great variety of bird life and some of the pools have been stocked with fish. The gravel extraction will continue until the end of the century but as the disused pits become filled and settled, some of the lakes are made available to the public. The lake complex covers an area from Pool Keynes, north of Ashton Keynes, to Cerney Wick, on to

Whelford, which relieves the congestion of the Marina at Lechlade. Sailing and fishing are already available at Keynes Park, swimming and power-boat racing at South Cerney, with tuition and equipment available. At Whelford, motorboat race meetings are held and adequate spectator and car parking facilities have been provided. For anyone with a good pair of field glasses, there are many

Kemble, well known to train enthusiasts for the elliptical arched bridges, designed by Isambard Brunel to take the line passing through Kemble Junction railway station

The South Cerney head, believed to be a relic of twelfth-century wood carving—possibly Spanish work brought home by a pilgrim from the shrine of St James at Santiago de Compostela

places in the quiet lanes from which to watch the water-fowl and a variety of other birds. The small ringed plovers have adopted the many lakes with their sandy shores which are preserved as bird sanctuaries. In addition to all this vast expanse of water in the new lakes, there are sections of the old canal to be found around Cricklade. Neglected and overgrown at the moment, they will surely be rescued by the many enthusiastic canal preservation societies. At Cerney Wick, the round house of the canal maintenance man is in good condition and is used as a cottage.

I went into Fairford by way of Down Ampney to visit the Old Vicarage, where the composer Vaughan Williams was born in 1872, and to see the memorial stone over the entrance carved by Simon Verity. In the church is the design for the new window to commemorate the R.A.F. squadrons which left Down Ampney aerodrome for the Normandy invasion. The church is at the end of a long driveway which leads to Down Ampney House, built in the fifteenth century, the home of the Hungerford families, some of whose monuments are in the church beside the thirteenth-century tombs of the de Valers.

Fairford is the most easterly of the wool towns, almost in the Thames valley, for at Lechlade, only a few miles away, the Cotswold rivers, the Coln and the Leach, flow into the Thames. The Saxons established a village there about A.D. 500. By the time of the Norman Conquest, it

Fairford

was for those times a densely populated area, with the villages splitting into separate settlements, which accounts for the three Ampneys. Fairford has developed into a busy market town with many elegant seventeenth- and eighteenth-century houses surrounding the market place. The restored Bull Hotel is well known to fishermen and used to be the headquarters for the meetings of the Thames and Severn Canal Company.

Near the entrance to the churchyard is the war memorial, Ernest Gimson's last design before his death and faithfully executed by the then young Norman Jewson. Beside the path leading to the church porch is a seat strategically placed to afford a good view of the beautiful exterior. The supports of this seat are fine examples of an early cast-iron design of rampant dragons supporting a cameo of a lady's head.

The church of St Mary at Fairford was completely rebuilt in 1490. The work was started by John Tame, a wool merchant, and completed by his son, Sir Edmund Tame. It is renowned for the twenty-eight windows with which John Tame tried to provide, in pictures, a summary of the Christian faith. They were designed at a time when few people could read, and he hoped the life of Christ depicted in the windows would educate his retainers and dependants as they worshipped in his church. The designs are based on the *Biblia Pauperum,* one of Europe's earliest illustrated books. The windows retain the original stained and painted glass, which is believed to have come from the workshops of Barnard Flower. Flower, who rose to be Master Glass Painter to Henry VII, employed the best of the English glass painters and also many French and Flemish artists. His workshops were responsible for the windows in the king's new Lady Chapel at Westminster Abbey and those at King's College, Cambridge. During the Second World War, the glass was removed from the church at Fairford and after the war, the windows were reglazed under the direction of Geoffrey Webb. The work was so well done that the windows proved strong enough to withstand the threatened shattering by the controversial Concorde aircraft, built only a few miles away. The twenty-eight windows cast a glowing light on the beautiful carving of the complete set of choir and parclose screens provided by Sir Edmund Tame and bearing the pomegranate emblem of Catherine of Aragon. Among the many memorials is one to the Rev. John Keble (1835) and his son John (1866).

I sat in a pew enjoying the full beauty of the interior; nothing disturbed my peace except the swish of a broom as the verger swept the floor. As I marvelled at the age and the state of preservation of the glass, the verger's cat jumped on my lap and purred his pleasure too. An elderly American couple finally disturbed the peace, as they rushed round the building with the guide-book, which with its excellent coloured photographs, certainly does justice to the windows. The lady stopped long enough in the centre aisle to exclaim "Oh Elmer! Oh my!", before making for the choir stalls, where she tipped up some of the amusingly carved misericords, saw a mouse, and called in a terrified voice for the verger. Peace reigned once more when the verger finally escorted them to the door.

"Pardon me, miss," he said, picking up the cat. As he departed towards the choir stalls I heard his reprimand: "I'm warning you, young Thomas, I'm not sweeping up after you. You take your own dead mice out of this church or you'll feel the end of my broom."

The exterior of the building creates an impression of extreme elegance, with the pierced stonework and the unusual coupled pinnacles on the tower. With the exception of the base of the central tower, which belongs to an older building, the church was entirely rebuilt by the Tame family in the last ten years of the fifteenth century. There are carvings on the walls of several figures and various coats of arms. The four grotesque demi-figures represent the guardians of the tower, to add a lighter touch the masons carved a boy scrambling over the string course. In addition to the arms of the lords of the manor, the Warwicks, the de Clares, the Despensers, there are the Tame's merchant's mark and various trade emblems

Fairford. Tudor Cottage, one of the few examples of half-timbering to be found in the Cotswolds

—shears and gloves, horseshoes and pincers and the shell of a salt trader.

Near the porch is the table tomb of Valentine Strong (1662), the church's master mason. He was the son of Thomas Strong of Taynton, who laid the foundation stone for Sir Christopher Wren's St Paul's Cathedral. His brother, Edward Strong, put the finishing touch to St Paul's by laying the last stone of the lantern, by which

193

time Sir Christopher was too old to climb to inspect the dome, but insisted on being hauled up in a mason's basket.

Valentine Strong was responsible for building Fairford Park, begun in 1661 for Andrew Barker and finally completed by his brother Thomas Strong. The old mansion was demolished some years ago and the town's secondary modern school was built on the site. Since no cars are allowed in the park, it is a pleasant place in which to walk.

Southrop

The River Coln was widened to form an ornamental water as it flows through the park. This ends at a stone bridge from which there is a popular view of the church, for the river rushes through the mill sluice-gates before widening yet again to flow along beside the church.

When the American artist E. A. Abbey was preparing the drawings for his mural depicting the landing of the Pilgrim Fathers in America, he worked in Fairford. He found the country folk in and around Fairford excellent models. When dressed in the costumes he provided, the faces assumed exactly the period look he had envisaged for his design. He was assisted in this great work at Philadelphia by the English painter, William Simmonds.

From Fairford, I turned north along the lanes towards Southrop and the Eastleaches for a late evening walk past Lappingwell Wood, in the hope of seeing a badger. You need time to sit and wait for a badger to come snuffling your way and the only time I have really seen one at close quarters was on a nearby farm. I was helping to dig out a fox which had taken to lurking in a temporary bolt-hole, from which it emerged to kill the farmer's new-born lambs. We dug first this way, then that, finding the zigzag route by probing with a drain rod from one bend to the next and digging at each bend. At last the rod met something soft—in went my friend's well-protected arm to pull out the offender. "Well, I'll be darned! All that work

Eastleach. Keble's bridge across the River Leach. This joined Eastleach
Turville and Eastleach Martin before the road bridge was constructed

for a sleepy old Mr Brock," he exclaimed, holding the badger for me to see before he sent him on his way.

The name Keble occurs in several of the villages near Fairford, for the Rev. John Keble was the vicar of St Aldwyn's and lived at Fairford. His two sons, John and Thomas, were his curates and for several years John Keble lived in the Old Vicarage at Southrop, where he held vacation reading parties for students from Oxford and entertained many learned friends, including William Gladstone who became Prime Minister. Edward Keble, a descendant of John, was appointed vicar of St Mary's, Fairford, in 1946.

Southrop is a quiet, unspoilt village of stone cottages and farm buildings. The church was built about 1100, replacing an earlier Saxon one. Although added to over the centuries, it was not ruined by the Victorian restorations. John Keble was curate there during 1823–5 and there is a memorial to a Thomas Keble (1670) which carries the Keble arms. The great treasure of the church is the font, elaborately carved with eight figures which represent Moses, the Church, the Synagogue and the Five Virtues—men with swords and shields trampling on five beast-like vices. These figures stand in trefoil arches with carved acanthus leaf and beaded interlacing above them. It was discovered by John Keble, built into the south doorway. The church was given to the Knights Hospitallers of St

John of Jerusalem, Clerkenwell, in the thirteenth century and they rebuilt the chancel and the transept. The altar tomb is thought to mask the entrance to a subterranean passage leading to the manor house. During Norman Jewson's alterations at the manor in 1926, a Norman archway was found near an underground chamber. The manor was granted to Newark College, Leicester, in the fourteenth century, but suppressed at the Dissolution, which accounts for the tradition that it was some kind of monastic house. The manor was bought in 1612 by Dorothy Wadham, founder of Wadham College, Oxford, and belonged to the college until 1926 when it was sold and modernized by Norman Jewson.

The way to the church is across the farmyard, between the manor and the stables—the porch has a stable-type door. At the far end of the farmyard is a small open-air museum with two old farm wagons filled with flowers, a cider press, a butter churn and a mangold chopper. There are also a number of trees, each planted in memory of a pony, in gratitude for the pleasure it had given its owner.

In 1690, the Keble family owned Grays Court, set back from the turning to Eastleach, now restored and renamed The Pines. It has a pleasant row of cottages, built from the old outhouses. The four-gabled dovecote with quoins and lantern belonged to Grays Court. Also topped by a lantern is the magnificent gabled barn with its great columbarium, which is to be seen south of the eighteenth-century Newman's House.

Spring is the ideal time to visit the Eastleach villages, which cling to the hillsides. There are some genuine old cottages, but those built when Eastleach Martin became part of the Hatherop estate of Sir Thomas Bazley in 1867 have weathered to become indistinguishable from the others. As you drop down to the River Leach in the spring, it is daffodils all the way, as in Wordsworth's lines—

> Ten thousand saw I at a glance,
> Tossing their heads in sprightly dance!

On either side of the river stand the two old churches, in close proximity because they were built at a time when the two hamlets belonged to different overlords. Eastleach Turville's church of St Andrew is recognizable by its small fourteenth-century saddleback tower. The south doorway is Norman work, with a fine tympanum and seats on either side of the porch from which to enjoy it. The interior contains a variety of different periods. The parishioners are rightly proud of the elm roof, which was made from local timber in 1906. The stand of the lectern, originally in Tewkesbury Abbey, served for some years as a stand for a parrot belonging to a Mrs Boyes Fowler.

After the death of the noble bird, she presented the stand to St Andrew's. One feels that it might have been fitting for the Bible to rest on the back of a parrot, rather than the conventional eagle.

John Keble was curate of both churches in 1815 and St Andrew's has a copy of his *Christian Year, Thoughts in verse for Sundays and Holy Days*. Several of these verses, including 'Blessed are the pure in heart', were set to music and have become popular hymns. The money from the sale of this little book, which went into ninety-two editions, enabled him to rebuild his church at Hursley, Hampshire. After his death there was sufficient to provide for a memorial—Keble College, Oxford. One wonders what this simple but brilliant man, a Scholar of Corpus Christi College at fourteen, Fellow of Oriel College at nineteen and a great admirer of the Cotswold style of building, would think of Keble College; whether he would approve of the ornate mid-Victorian brick building and the recent glass and steel addition?

In front of the altar of St Andrew's is a beautifully embroidered carpet, one of the unsung treasures so often to be found in village churches. The design, by H. P. Hewell, based on a seventeenth-century carpet, was embroidered by members of the Oxford Embroidery Group, and although made up of fourteen panels worked in separate homes, it shows no sign of joins nor is there any apparent disparity in the work. In the churchyard is a small grave-stone, with a fine modern head of Christ incised on it, surmounting this a gay little lead cherub. It is a beautiful memorial to a young relative of a famous playwright.

Keble's Bridge, an old stone clapper footbridge across the Leach, is thought by many to have been named after John Keble, who crossed it so often when he was a curate, but Kebles lived here in the sixteenth century and they held Eastleach Turville Manor for five generations.

St Michael and St Martin's, the church which stands on the opposite side of the river, was founded by Richard Fitzpons, who came to Britain with the Conqueror. He was one of five brothers, and in memory of this had five sundials placed on his church. He made a deed of gift of the church to the Priory at Malvern; a copy of this twelfth-century deed and that of a gift of land in South-rop, dated 1134, are still preserved and may be seen in the British Museum.

Tyley Bottom. The footpath from Symonds Hall Farm, through Tyley Bottom, past the lake, leads to the lane into Coombe. The hamlet of Coombe has a terrace of weavers' cottages and Coombe House, although rebuilt, retains the ancient rubble chimney-stacks

CHAPTER ELEVEN

Bradwell and Burford to Moreton-in-Marsh

A secondary road leads from the sheltered Eastleigh valley way over the windy Broughton and Filkin Downs to Bradwell. This lovely estate now houses the Cotswold Wildlife Park. Apart from the collection of animals, excellent aviaries and an enclosure for otters, it offers an opportunity to walk in the grounds. The park, which extends over 3,500 acres, has been farmed and afforested for centuries. The present house, Bradwell Grove, is early nineteenth-century Gothic, built on the site of a Jacobean manor house. The trees are magnificent; one oak tree near the restaurant is 400 years old and many of the other well-established trees in the park were planted when the house was built.

At the foot of Westhall Hill and Burford's High Street, the River Windrush winds and twists its leisurely way to join the Thames. Its valley narrows here between the hills, which on one side rise up towards Stow and on the other is the steep street which climbs through Burford to the ridge road. In A.D. 752 there was no bridge across the Windrush, the fierce battle between the Kings of Mercia and Wessex was fought across a ford. A bridge is first recorded in 1322, when bridge tolls were collected in the reign of Edward II. At that time, tolls were paid on a surprising variety of goods destined for Burford market. These included dried fish from Aberdeen, dress materials from France, linen from Ireland, foreign wines, local cider and metals from Birmingham. Nearly one hundred years later, liberty to build a new bridge was granted by King Henry V and the work was commissioned by one John of Helens, who in his will left money for its maintenance. For most of its history Burford has been a fortunate town. In the reign of William II, the manor of Burford was given to FitzHamon, who lived at Tewkesbury. Rather than travel to Burford to collect his taxes, he gave the inhabitants a charter to hold markets, a fair and a court to collect dues and fines payable to FitzHamon. This charter was confirmed by Henry II, by Edward III and again by Henry VI. Burford did not suffer so much from the wool and cloth depressions which afflicted many of the Cotswold towns and villages. It was the general market town for a wide area, where merchants lived, dealing in a large variety of goods. It has had its ups and downs but has never suffered from acute poverty, disease, or unemployment. This is reflected in the state of preservation of the old buildings which line its streets. Once over the narrow bridge, the High Street has always been exceptionally wide, to accommodate the market and the fairs.

There are conflicting reports about what happened to the bridge in 1797. One report says it was badly damaged by a freak storm which flooded the Windrush, another that it was wilfully damaged to prevent foreign cheeses being brought into Burford Fair. Whatever the cause, after repairs and underpinning it still carries the traffic which crosses it today.

In country lore, St Valentine's Day is the time the birds start their courting and is known as the birds' wedding day. The wider reaches of the Windrush are used by swans each year, for nesting and rearing their cygnets. The jack-daws favour the church tower, as the builders soon know when they go up there for repair work. During World War II, the fifteenth-century bridge took a battering from the heavy commercial vehicles which crossed it—or failed to do so. A Sherman tank plunged through the parapet into the river and on another occasion, I was driving be-hind a 70-foot-long vehicle used for transporting crashed aeroplanes (known in R.A.F. slang as Queen Marys). The driver miscalculated the turn on to the bridge and his cab dived into the river leaving his back wheels on the road. By the time I reached the lorry, he had managed to open the door of his submerged cab and was climbing, wet and dripping, up the side of his lorry. Shocked and shaken, he leaned against the parapet of the bridge to recover, then suddenly exclaimed—"The kids' sweet ration!" (During the war, sweets were severely rationed and most grown-ups kept theirs for children.) To my horror, he slid down the side of the lorry and disappeared under the swirling water into his cab. He emerged with a happy smile on his face and climbed back to the bridge, saying: "Lucky thing I bought them paper-wrapped toffees" as he ignored his condition and we carefully dried the sweets with my car duster.

During the last few years, there have been several schemes for a bypass, with a bridge further up the river, in order to relieve the present bridge and free the High Street from the heavy traffic, which is damaging some of the old roofs, causing the tile-stones to be shaken off their wooden or sheep-bone pegs by traffic vibration. But there is so much beautiful country along the Windrush valley that the best solution might be the suggested longer detour by heavy vehicles along existing roads. In the mean-

Burford, recorded in the Domesday survey as a 'Riverside burh' with church, mills and houses. The popular name today is 'The Gateway to the Cotswolds'

time, the ancient bridge bears up under the load, relieved to some extent by traffic lights which permit only one lane of traffic at a time. These lights were installed after a high lorry, trying to pass a car, took the oriel window off the house called Mouseham.

On the left, before approaching the bridge, is Cocklands House, home of the Cocklands Press, where the wood-engraver, Helen Bryce, printed her delightful greetings cards. She died in 1971, but the press continues to print the cards. I went in for a new supply and for a chance to look through the window across the garden to Ladyham. I had heard about the house from Fay Compton, the actress, and how her brother Monty (Compton Mackenzie) and his cousin, Christopher Stone, students at Oxford, tried to rent Ladyham, a much altered Elizabethan house which at that time belonged to a Mr Sylvester whose ancestors had built the Lady Chapel in the church across the river. The property was called Lady Ham, meaning "Our Lady's field by the water". The mill stream and the River Windrush separated the churchyard from the Sylvester land, flowed round the back of the house and served the outdoor privy. After arranging to rent part of his house, Mr Sylvester had a stroke in his garden, fell into the river and was drowned. The two young undergraduates were then faced with buying the whole property—the house up the drive and the two houses by the bridge, Mouseham and Mr Sylvester's grocer's shop. By various means, they managed to raise the money and when they came to alter the main house they found the original deeds, dated 1585, behind the plaster of one of the walls.

The church of St John the Baptist, across the river from Ladyham, built of local stone, was begun in the reign of Henry II. An excellent illustrated guide is available, giving the history of the building and mentioning the visit in 1876 of William Morris, the founder of The Society for the Protection of Ancient Buildings, nicknamed the Anti-Scrape Society. He was on his way to visit Cornell Price at Broadway Tower when he noticed Burford church was being restored. He was horrified to see the alterations which were being made, remonstrated with the vicar, the Rev. W. A. Cass, who resented his interference and eventually told him, "The church, sir, is mine and if I choose to, I shall stand on my head in it!" One hopes he chose to do this on the new floor tiles which Morris disliked so much.

Appreciation and preservation of old buildings is no longer left to the far-sighted few. 1975 was the European Architectural Heritage year, when grants for a variety of improvements were given. Many Cotswold authorities, including Burford, had their plans ready; the grant enabled the council to provide new pavements and excellent street lighting, strategically placed to flood-light the buildings.

Near the church are the Church Green almshouses, given by Warwick the Kingmaker when he was Lord of the Manor of Burford, an interesting row of buildings which, carefully repaired, demonstrate the craft of the stonemason in the late 1400s. The small green in front, with its seat and single tree, has been reduced in size to allow for new roads which enable visitors to reach the free car park on the far side of the Windrush; a good place from which to watch the water voles, swans and small waterfowl, the willows and the water meadows, before walking back to the High Street.

A studio stands below the bridge, which has been used by stonemasons for many years. I knew Edgar Frith, a sculptor and stone cutter, who always wore a square newspaper hat to protect his hair from stone dust, reminding one of Tenneil's drawing of the Carpenter in *Alice in Wonderland*. He retired some years ago, but Mr Collett is carrying on the tradition of the Windrush Studio. He allowed me to walk in his yard amongst the great blocks of stone from various Cotswold quarries to admire the incredible variety of their ochre colours and textures.

Burford has always been busy with traffic, and in the coaching era, the South Wales, Hereford and Gloucester coaches passed through Burford on their way to London

Burford. Historical beasts outside one of the town's many antique shops

and back. In those days the A40, at the top of the hill, did not exist. The coach route along Sheep Street and Witney Street was the top of the town. In their heyday, as many as forty coaches passed through Burford in a day. The warning notes of their long copper horns brought out the ostlers and stable boys to handle packages and rub down the horses. The passengers stretched their legs and went in search of the appetizing meals provided by the many inns.

The saying "Beware of taking a Burford Bait" was a warning not to overeat. Though stuffy and uncomfortable inside, the coaches were gaily painted outside and displayed their names and routes—The Magnet and the Berkeley from Cheltenham, the Mazeppa and the Rapid from Hereford, the Regulator and the Retaliator from Gloucester.

The oldest part of Burford lies between the bridge and Sheep Street. Cob Hall, so called because it was once the Swan Inn, was first recorded in 1590. Now privately owned, it was at one period the Boys' National School, recently rehoused in a building round the corner, by the priory. The earliest record of what is called the priory was in 1226, when it was a small Augustinian hospital, kept by a master and three brethren to afford shelter for sick people and travellers. Following the Dissolution, it had several owners up to the time when Sir Lawrence Tanfield built a large Elizabethan house on the site. This house has had many distinguished visitors—James I, Charles II with Nell Gwynne, and William III. King William stayed there when Lord Abercorn was the owner. The latter was the stepfather of the two grandsons of William Lenthall, Speaker of the Long Parliament and for many years owner of the priory. Lord Abercorn was accused of the murder of the boys' trustee, John Prior, whose body was found hidden in a summerhouse in the garden. With the help of influential friends, the charge against Lord Abercorn was dismissed but the murderer was never found. Many ghostly visitations have been recorded at the priory and when Lady Southby lived there, after a further restoration, she was convinced the old house would have no peace until it was returned to the church.

When Compton Mackenzie was at Ladyham, the priory was empty and is described in his novel *Guy and Pauline*: "the great pile . . . brooded in the silence with a monstrous ghostliness . . . the casements, whose glass was filmy, like the eyes of dead men . . . ."

In 1947, it was acquired by the church and twenty sisters of the Benedictine Order live there. At first, they were disturbed by the figure of a man dressed as a gamekeeper, who the nuns thought was someone from the town, until he walked through a wall and disappeared. They also saw a monk dressed in a brown habit, heard singing in the garden by the monks' burial ground, and the sound of a bell, ringing at 2 a.m., the time when medieval monks were called to prayer. The nuns found it disturbing when they first arrived, but the priory and the grounds have remained peaceful during the last few years.

The lane above the priory leads up into Sheep Street, with its variety of old houses. On the corner facing the High Street is the Tolsey, a room built on stone pillars, where the tolls were paid. This now houses a small museum, including a doll's house, the idea of Helen Bryce, who persuaded some of the local craftsmen to join together and supply scale models of their own particular crafts. F. Russell Cox, the Burford architect, designed the façade being inspired by the Great House in Witney Street. Helen Bryce made and dressed the figures in the doll's house and the beautiful table glass and chandeliers were the work of the Methodist minister, whose somewhat unusual hobby was working with malleable glass.

Further along Sheep Street is the home of *The Countryman*, the country magazine started by that prolific writer on all country matters, J. W. Robertson Scott. In 1927, during one of the many agricultural depressions, he retired from the editorial staff of the *Pall Mall Gazette* and went to live at Idbury Manor. Here he wrote his classic, *England's Green and Pleasant Land*. On the front of his house he had had carved in stone the Virgilian words, "Oh more than happy countryman, if he but knew his good fortune", a view he tried to encourage through the medium of his magazine *The Countryman*. He launched a campaign for better living conditions for country workers and fought to prevent the urbanization of the countryside. His magazine was an immediate success and soon achieved a world-wide circulation. He was the editor for twenty years but it was not until 1947 that *The Countryman* moved to premises in Sheep Street, under the editorship of John Stafford Cripps. The building, like most of the properties in Sheep Street, has a long and varied history. In the coaching era, it was the Greyhound Inn, in the railway era, Mr Paintin's Temperance Hotel, where he kept the horse buses which ran to Shipton-under-Wychwood three times a day. Now, the editor's private house is at the rear, while Mr Paintin's oak-floored, beamed dining-room has become a reception room for *The Countryman's* visitors. A portrait of Robertson Scott hangs above the handsome stone fireplace, made by Mr Collett at the Windrush Studio.

There are many short cul-de-sacs off the High Street, which contains some beautiful smaller houses. One leads from the wide archway of the George Hotel and has ten cottages, which have been carefully restored and modernized for renting to Burford people. As in so many Cotswold villages, too much property has been acquired since the last war to serve as 'second houses' for people who come for weekends. This tends to destroy a village community and makes property too expensive for the rightful inhabitants, who as at Burford are often housed on council estates a long way from their shops. This situation is described in Frank Mansell's poem 'The Cottager's Reply', addressed to a would-be purchaser offering more than his cottage was worth. The last four lines of the poem read:

So take your glass and drain it down,
You would-be peasant from the town,
Go on your journey, let me bide
Contented in my own countryside.

Continuing along Sheep Street towards Upton is Kit's Quarry. The house was built by Christopher Kempster, one of the Cotswolds' most famous masons. He quarried stone from the Upton hillside for Sir Christopher Wren, for use on the many buildings which he was commissioned to build after the Great Fire of London, including St Paul's Cathedral. Kempster was eager to learn from Wren, who described him as "modest and treatable". Kempster also applied his knowledge and skill to improving the buildings in his home town and eventually built for his own retirement a house on the floor of the quarry he had excavated. This was in 1698 and his descendants continued to live there until 1885. Later, it was the home of the writer, C. E. Montague, who in the peace of Kit's Quarry House, high above the Windrush valley, wrote his powerful books about World War I. The house has been carefully restored and modernized by F. Russell Cox, its present owner, who is architect to the parish church. I am sure that no Burford vicar in his time will feel the need to stand on his head. Surrounding Kit's Quarry House are the old quarries, overgrown with hawthorns, as they have not been worked since the end of the eighteenth century. Now, their five acres protect the garden from the noise of the traffic on the ridge road.

I left busy, bustling Burford to return to Great Barrington, in the hope of a talk with William Hall and his son Brian. The Hall family, like the Baldwins at Rodmarton, have been smiths in the village of Great Barrington for generations. They, too, are overwhelmed with agricul-

Icomb. A small village near Icomb Place, a handsome house rebuilt about 1420, probably by Sir John Blaket, whose magnificent monument is in the village church

tural repairs, which leaves them little time for any creative work.

"I did manage enough time to make a pair of gates for the Fox Inn, down in the valley and we do some interesting church work for the big firms which undertake restorations, but," Bill said in his soft Cotswold drawl, "we get no credit for that."

I told him I was going on to Taynton to see if Mr Lee had time to walk round the quarries with me.

"I doubt it," said Bill Hall, "he's like the rest of us, run off his feet. I'll tell you this though, don't you make him an offer to buy the quarry lands, like a big-business chap did last week, or you'll be seen off with a gun!"

Bill Hall was right, Mr Philip Lee certainly was rushed off his feet. It had been cattle inspection day and the regular farm work was all behind, but he had no objection to my walking up to his quarries.

"I'm all behind with my stone-cutting too," was his parting shot, as he rushed out towards the barn to load his tractor. I lingered on in the farm porch to examine the pile of fossils, collected from the quarries over many years. There were pieces of rock containing small cavities of sparkling calcite crystals, shells of various types and bits of coral—the deposits of the ancient sea bed, elevated millions of years ago to form the oolitic limestone of the Cotswold Hills.

Idbury. Here J. W. Robertson Scott wrote his classic "England's Green and Pleasant Land"

It is an uphill but historically interesting climb from the Lees' sixteenth-century farmhouse, through the quarry lands, which for centuries brought work to Burford. They lie on the Taynton side of the Windrush, between the Stow road and the deep combe made by the Hazelford Brook, as it flows down from Tangley Woods to join the Windrush. The hillside is scarred with quarry workings and gruffy ground left after the removal of tile-stones. A quarry was mentioned here in the Domesday survey, and

207

in the ten years following 1358, 2,000 tons of stone were quarried for the enlarging of Windsor Castle, at a time when Richard of Taynton was the clerk of the works there to Edward III's chaplain, William of Wykeham.

Stone from Taynton was supplied for the medieval Oxford colleges. In the seventeenth and eighteenth centuries, Strongs of Taynton sent stone to London for the Wren buildings and to Fairford for the church and the manor house. The stone for Blenheim Palace was quarried from Lee's quarry, which also supplied stone for the New Bodleian Library at Oxford. Rally quarry provided stone for the railway bridges built over the River Evenlode in 1846. Except for Lee's quarry, from which Mr Lee supplies stone for repair work, the old workings are overgrown with trees and wild flowers. At first, the region seemed silent and deserted, as I rested on a block of stone, but the birds and small creatures must have waited for me to pass or to sit quietly before they resumed their rightful business. The rabbits came out to feed among the cowslips, a mole emerged from a heap of earth, looked round as if to say "I am the little black lord of the underworld, proud and solitary in my tight plush". He did not like the daylight and hastily dug his way back underground. There were pheasants and partridges on the rough grassland, ignoring the fieldfares which came in small flocks to join them. Greenfinches were enjoying the knapweed and the green woodpeckers sent out their mocking call from the woods behind, as I looked out over the vast expanse of uplands. I disagree with Sidney Smith's description of these as, "a region of stone and sorrow . . . abandoned to the screaming kites and larcenous crows". The crows were there, but alas, no kites; they are rarely seen outside Wales, where they have their own warden. Their place was taken by the plovers, rising and falling, playing games in the thermals, undisturbed by my return to the valley below, to Mr Lee's stone-cutting yard. I was not left in peace for long to enjoy the warm colours of the freshly worked stone contrasting with the grey of the weathered pieces. A herd of inquisitive, playful bullocks came up to help me on my way. I am content to be the loser in bullocks' games and beat a hasty retreat behind the safety of the field gate.

I drove over the wolds towards Moreton-in-Marsh, taking the lane through Idbury. Here almost opposite Robertson Scott's manor house is the church, with its elegant pinnacled bell turret and a small brass to the Taynton stonemason Thomas Hautin, who died in 1653. This brass is crudely engraved to show a mason's axe and bolster, and a naïve, cheerful portrait of Thomas.

The village of Bledington has a large rectangular green, with a maypole around which the village children dance on festive occasions. Through the centuries Bledington

Bledington. After World War I Cecil Sharp recovered and recorded many country dances and tunes, including "Bledington Hey Away"

Adelstrop. The church of St Mary Magdalene

has housed some highly skilled masons, particularly in the fifteenth century, as witness the elaborate work in the church of St Leonard. This may be because the advowson belonged to the wealthy abbots of Winchcombe; Manor Farm is said to be on the site of a rest house used by the monks of Winchcombe. Also in the church are traces of wall paintings and fragments of glass thought to have been made by John Prudde of Westminster, well known as the glazier of the windows in the Beauchamp Chapel in Warwick. In view of the grandeur of the church, one gets the impression that Bledington might have been destined for development into a more important place but for Henry VIII and his confiscation of the wealth of the monasteries. There are several good stone houses and regrettably, some of brick, the product of a brick works which was once in the village. An excellent walk and bridle-path leads across Bledington Heath to Oddington.

The village of Lower Oddington was built in the early eighteenth century on higher ground than an earlier village. The Saxon settlement was beside a tributary of the Evenlode—on old maps marked as the Odyn. This village was abandoned in the early 1700s, when most of the inhabitants died of a vicious plague which swept through Gloucestershire. A church was built in the new village, following which the old church of St Nicholas gradually became derelict. Fortunately, before it was beyond repair,

a restoration grant was received in 1920. It is approached by a narrow lane leading from the main street, or from the bridle-path crossing Bledington Heath. For those who enjoy the horrors of the early Doom artists, a visit to this church will prove rewarding, for the torments of the damned are portrayed with diabolical realism. They are shown as being cooked in cauldrons stirred by fearsome monsters, but the redeemed manage to struggle up to Heaven, depicted as a well-fortified castle. One exhausted climber is being hauled over the battlements by a kind but busy angel. Among the other paintings is that of a preaching fox—a popular medieval jibe at Franciscan friars. It is an odd coincidence that while the church was derelict, a vixen chose to raise her cubs in the shelter of the richly carved Jacobean pulpit.

The small hamlet of Adlestrop, the church, the rectory, the schoolhouse and the cottages are built in a corner of Adlestrop Park. This was a monastic property of Evesham Abbey until it came into the possession of the Leigh family. Many readers of Jane Austen visit this corner of the Cotswolds. Her great-uncle, Theophilus Leigh, a dry humorist who for fifty years was Master of Balliol College, Oxford, was also Rector of Adlestrop from 1718 to 1762. Jane and her mother Cassandra (*née* Leigh) were staying with her uncle Thomas Leigh in 1806, when he received the news that he had inherited Stoneleigh Abbey, the Warwickshire seat of the Leigh family. Jane and her mother went with him to view his inheritance and it was at Stoneleigh that Jane is reputed to have written some of her novels. The gardens at Adlestrop Park, with sweeping lawns and a lake fed by a small tributary of the Evenlode, were designed by Humphrey Repton; they are, alas, no longer open to the public. A public footpath crosses the park from Daylesford, in which one can see a little of the tree planting of Repton, who, like the landscape gardener William Kent,

> Calls in the country, catches opening glades,
> Joins willing woods and varies shades with shades.

The railway station at Adlestrop, no longer a public one, was once well known to readers of the poet Edward Thomas, whose train "stopped unwontedly at Adlestrop".

The Iron Age people, thought to have numbered between one and two million in England, have left few traces of their occupation. On the wolds above Adlestrop is an indication of one of their circular forts, The Roundabout. There are several walks over the hill, and the lane from the A436 to Chastleton House passes near to the fort. Chastleton House is a Jacobean building which has undergone little alteration, inside or out, since it was built. In the year Queen Elizabeth I died, Walter Jones, a

Member of Parliament, bought the estate from Robert Catesby, later one of the Gunpowder Plot conspirators, who had already become impoverished by a heavy fine for his part in the Essex rebellion. Walter's elegant house was nearing completion when his eldest son, Henry, married the wealthy Anne Fettiplace from Painswick. There was a rhyme of that time—

> The Tracys, the Lacys and Fettiplaces,
> Own all the best manors, the woods and the chases.

This expressed the resentment of the poor when these wealthy families chose to make enclosures which robbed them of their small strips of land. There was no redress— they had to suffer the alternatives of starving or begging.

One of the many interesting items to be seen in Chastleton House (which is open daily to the public) is the Bible of Charles I, which he gave to Bishop Juxon on the morning of his execution. The Juxons owned Little Compton Manor, about a mile from Chastleton. The Bible, printed in 1629, and bearing the royal arms and cypher on the binding, was given by the last of the Juxons into the safe keeping of their royalist neighbours at Chastleton.

Arthur, grandson of Walter Jones, fled from the Battle of Worcester in 1651, reached home and hid in a secret hiding place. His pursuers found a tired horse in the stables but searched the house without success. They decided to stay for the night and chose the bedroom which connected with the hide-hole. His wife doped their supper beer with opium and rescued her husband while the soldiers slept. Arthur cavalierly rode off on one of his pursuers' best horses.

From the windows of the long gallery at the top of the house are extensive views of the agricultural countryside and of Chastleton's rare topiary garden. From above it is possible to see the overall design of the garden, which was laid out when William of Orange made this idea so popular with the English. Like the house, it has remained unaltered; though the shapes of the birds and beasts, the ship, the crown and the box hedges have been well developed over the centuries. Alexander Pope, a keen toparian, records some topiary bargains offered him by a nurseryman: "A pair of giants—stunted." "To be sold cheap, Edward the Black Prince in cypress," "Noah's Ark in holly, the ribs a little damaged for want of water".

Overlooking the topiary garden is the small Norman church of St Mary the Virgin, which contains a brass to Katherine Throckmorton, grandmother of Robert Catesby, whose only son's baptism is recorded in the registers, which date back to 1575. The views from the Long Gallery were all the Stuart ladies saw of the surrounding country, as they took their daily walk up and down the

room. It was considered neither safe nor genteel for them to walk in the country.

I stopped at Evenlode to see the work of a potter who has revived the art of old English slipware. It was intriguing to watch the artist drawing the traditional designs freehand in liquid clay. "Simple," she explained, "Just like icing a cake."

Evenlode. In the eighth century land at Evenlode was leased by the Abbot of Gloucester for the payment of a hundred sheep

The clay flowed into the paint brush from a rubber container called a 'trailer'—rather like the bulb of an old-fashioned motor horn. It did not flow for me—it burst forth in a series of abominable blobs. Months of practice must obviously be needed to give just the right pressure. I asked the potter, a German, how he came to settle in Evenlode. This caused much merriment among his fellow workers, as I gathered he had come to England in order to marry a potter's daughter, the lady who was so skilled in decorating his slipware.

Across the River Evenlode is Broadwell and the restored church of St Paul, which still retains carved Saxon stones and a Maltese cross in the beautiful tympanum. Outstanding among the monuments are the alabaster effigies of the Westons (1635), the classical stone to Robert Hunkes (1585), and a late heraldic brass to Piers Thursby (1904), who built Broadwell Hill House in 1879. Attractive seventeenth-century buildings and farmhouses surround the extremely large green, with a long line of pollarded willows beside the stream and the ford.

There are several versions of the origin of the name Moreton-in-Marsh. Some historians believe it was a march or frontier, similar to the Welsh Marches, and marked by four Saxon stones. In the eighteenth century, the Four Shires stone replaced them and marked the boundaries of four counties, now incorrect since the formation of new counties in 1931. This stone stands on the corner of the A44, where it is joined by the lane to Great Wolford. The town was founded by the Abbey of Westminster in 1226, beside the Fosse Way where the latter was crossed by the road connecting Worcester, Oxford and London. It was surrounded at one time by low-lying land called Hen Marsh, a favourite haunt of moorhens. According to old records, this part of the Fosse Way was sometimes flooded, which may explain the present name. With the building of the railway, the Fosse Way was raised in 1868, to reduce the gradient to the railway bridge, and the surrounding fields were drained so 'in-Marsh' is no longer applicable.

Moreton-in-Marsh is on the edge of Cotswold country, near enough to be used by commuters from the South Midlands and London. At the east end of the main street, many of the buildings are of red brick with slate roofs. In this street, one of the widest in the Cotswolds, George VI reviewed the Airborne Division in 1944 before the Normandy landings.

The Redesdale Hall, which occupies an island site in this wide street, was built as recently as 1887 and presented to the town by Lord Dulverton of Batsford. The oldest building, difficult to identify as it tops the service station on the corner of Oxford Street, is the Curfew Tower, at one time the town 'lock-up'. The bell, dated 1633, was

Moreton-in-Marsh, a popular commuter town, difficult to maintain as a village community

rung daily until 1860. The oldest part of the town was the area around the church, which was almost completely rebuilt in 1858 and the Old Parsonage is now marred by a Welsh slate roof.

Moreton is rightly proud of its Fire Service Technical College, one of the largest and most advanced in Europe.

The Manor House Hotel dates from 1658, and opposite are the workshops of Hugh Birkett, whose cabinet-making I had admired at Rodmarton Manor, where some workboxes were so accurately made that the small interior boxes would only sink gently into place as the displacement of air allowed. Here is an original designer whose fine craftsmanship follows the traditions of the Sapperton Group. At Rodmarton Manor I had also seen the work of Oliver Morel, remarkable raised inlaid panels in a beautifully made display cabinet. Hundreds of minute pieces of carefully selected unstained wood of different types had been chosen to create the delicate flower pictures, including the rarer wild flowers and butterflies to be found near Rodmarton and the spotted fly-catchers which for many years have nested in the creeper outside the dining-room window of the Manor. He showed me similar exquisite pieces in his workshop at Moreton. Seeing and handling rare and perfect pieces of craftsmanship in any material gives me as much pleasure as seeing some of the recognized "Art Treasures of the World".

O
MORE THAN
HAPPY
COVNTRYMAN
IF
HE·BVT·KNEW
HIS·GOOD
FORTVNE

Idbury. The plaque which J. W. Robertson Scott placed on his house,
a quotation from Virgil

Hidcote Garden, showing one of the elegant gazebos and the well-developed stilt hedge. Beyond the handsome wrought-iron gates is a view across the Vale of Evesham to Bredon Hill

CHAPTER TWELVE

The Cotswold Gardens

Christ save Henry the Eighth, our royal King,
The Red rose in honour to flourish and spring!

The rose became the emblem of England at the time of the Tudors, since when the English have steadily developed into a nation of gardeners. Posterity has received some benefit from the Dissolution of the Monasteries, for the astute courtiers of Henry's time became the *nouveaux riches*. With the money and lands which came their way, they were able to build for themselves 'The stately homes of England'. It soon became fashionable to surround their houses with gardens as well as parks, and ideas were copied from the Italians and, later, from the great gardens of Versailles. Here, André le Nôtre, son and grandson of master gardeners, was lavishly laying out the palace gardens for the extravagant 'Sun King', Louis XIV. In England, John Evelyn and Sir Thomas More wrote about gardens and gardening. In his *Utopia*, More wrote:

They set great store by their gardens . . . their study and diligence herein cometh not only from pleasure but also a certain strife and contention that is between street and street, concerning the trimming, husbanding and furnishing of their gardens . . . the first founder of the city minded nothing so much as he did these gardens.

Written in 1518, this part of his *Utopia* has become very true today, when city architects, town planners and motorway engineers have added landscaping to their list of requirements.

My interest in gardening began when I was old enough to claim a ride on the rubbish I had piled into my father's enormous elm wheelbarrow. My first pocket money was earned by sweeping paths and often lost through searching for a ball in a precious flower bed. My school friend and fellow gardener is Alice Coates, who has written many books on the history of plants, and has been awarded the last Gold Medal to be given by the Royal Horticultural Society—(the last gold, because from now on they are to be silver-gilt). As young gardeners we both studied the work of Gertrude Jeykell (1843–1932). Miss Jeykell was a garden designer with an artist's true sense of colour and a subtle choice of plants for colour effect. She was a friend and colleague of the architect Edwin Lutyens, who was responsible for the landscaping of the gardens at Abbots-wood, near Stow-on-the-Wold. The planting was undertaken by the owner, the great horticulturalist Mark Fennick. I never walk round this beautiful estate with its magnificent lawns, flower beds, creeper-covered walls, water garden and wild shrubberies, without feeling that the subtle influence of Gertrude Jeykell was behind the plans of the two men. As all garden lovers will know, her advice and her writings helped to create England's finest gardens, including those at Wisley, the Saville Gardens at Windsor, and those at Bodnant and Nymans. The Lutyens memorial to her at Busbridge carries this simple inscription, which perhaps best describes this remarkable lady, who stood alone as the great woman gardener of her day.

ARTIST

GARDENER

CRAFTSWOMAN

The idea of opening private gardens to the public originated in the desire to perpetuate the memory of Queen Alexandra, who was the patron of the Queen's Institute of District Nursing. Since 1927, when the National Gardens Scheme was inaugurated, the number of gardens open has increased by hundreds each year and now includes the royal gardens. Many are open several times during the season and some villages try to arrange that all their best gardens are open on the same day. Whether or not you have gardening interests, this is often a rare opportunity of seeing the best in the Cotswold villages: to walk in and out of the gardens, a welcome guest; to see the beauty of the stone buildings from all sides, manor and cottage alike; to walk along simple garden paths or through great parks and along stretches of beautiful river often flanked by water gardens.

At Alderley Grange is one of the best of the smaller Cotswold gardens. It is packed with rare plants and carefully designed to take the visitor from one breath-taking vista to another. This garden, like many others, is open on a Monday in addition to the weekend, which gives retired people a chance to enjoy them at leisure. The garden at The Grange, apart from the walls and large trees, has been designed and created since 1962 by Mrs Lees-Milne. Inspired by the work of Marianne North of Alderley, she has acquired her horticultural knowledge from an intense interest, observation and sheer hard work. From the Georgian summerhouse set in the highest corner of the lawn is a view of the roses, which include a bed of the brilliant white Icebergs, the carefully planted trees and the rare climbers on the high wall which leads to the herb garden. This has a formal layout, with beds radiating from a stone column which supports an armillary sphere. The narrow brick paths are edged with dwarf box sheltering a near-complete collection of English herbs.

The 'Long Walk' in the garden is bordered on one side by a hedge of the older shrub roses 'Rosa Mundi' is described in one catalogue as a rose with "long and elegant hips" another variety "does better in a bed than against a wall"! Pleached limes perfume the air along a walk which leads to a vista of an eighteenth-century marble statue of Apollo with his lyre. Behind this is a mass of tall, dark green shrubs and at the foot, a riot of greys and yellows. The back drive and the surround of the front lawn have been planted with rare, decorative trees, carefully selected and placed for all-the-year-round colour. A covenant for this garden has been accepted by the National Trust, so no major alterations may take place in the future.

One is rather spoilt for choice at the joint opening of village gardens, particularly those at Quenington, for then it is possible to see Quenington Mill, the Old Rectory, the River House and many other beautiful buildings in their natural surroundings, instead of having to be satisfied with a fleeting glimpse from a road.

Quenington Court was built on the site of the Precep-tory of the Knights Hospitallers, completed by them in 1193. Although the present house is nineteenth century, the dovecote is fourteenth century and the gatehouse with its postern doorway is believed to be the original entrance used by the Knights. The church is dedicated to St Swithun, who for ten years was Bishop of Winchester (852–862), during which time he was tutor to the young son of Ethelwulf, the boy who became Alfred the Great, the first king of all the English. This village church is well known for its two Norman doorways and the carving of the Coronation of the Virgin, one of the earliest depicting this subject. Quenington like other villages competes for the Bledisloe Cup, awarded to the best-kept village of the year.

At Barnsley House, David and Rosemary Verey open their garden several times a year. David Verey is the architectural historian, author of the volume on Gloucestershire and the Cotswolds in the series 'Buildings of England'. Rosemary is at work on a mammoth book tracing the history of Cotswold gardens from the time of the Romans. They delight in showing the many visitors their latest plants raised from roots, bulbs, seeds and cuttings brought from abroad. This is allowed provided you leave this country with the necessary permit, obtainable from the Ministry of Agriculture. On one open day, we talked on a seat shaded on one side by a small tree grown from a seed brought from Madrid—a *Gleditschia triacanthus*, first cousin to the acacia. On the other side was a *Paulonia*, brought from the botanical gardens in Padua. One greenhouse was full of seeds, cuttings and plants brought from a trip to Ethiopia. Rosemary Verey believes in planting trees and shrubs which give the maximum value all through the season, with their flowers, leaves and berries. Among the many beds of beautiful flowers is a bed of woad, *Isatis tinctoria*, which was used as a dye for the Cotswold wool industry.

Barnsley House has a date-stone 1697 and stands almost in the centre of the garden. The eighteenth-century Gothic Alcove is in its original position, though it seems to belong more to the pseudo-Gothic style of Horace Walpole's house, Strawberry Hill, than to a Cotswold garden. The Tuscan Doric Temple (1787) at the opposite end of the garden was moved from Fairford Park in 1962. It serves as a summerhouse from which to enjoy the vista between the herbaceous borders beyond the ornamental pool to the fountain by Simon Verity at the far end. On a small column by the fountain is a plate engraved by him.

The estate which is now Batsford Park near Moreton-in-Marsh is known to have belonged to the Freeman family from 1500, possibly earlier. The gardens and arboretum were created by A. B. Freeman-Mitford, first

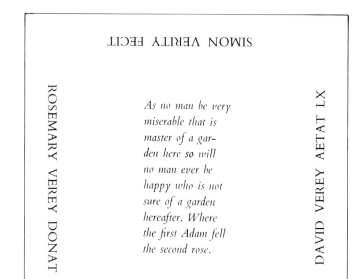

Batsford arboretum. Here the Buddha sits under an oak tree beside the incense cedars, a palm tree at least eighty years old and a Californian nutmeg tree

Baron Redesdale (1837–1916). He was a member of the Foreign Office and spent many years in Asia, China and Japan, which experience is reflected in the design and planting of his gardens. He always said he owed his inspiration to the natural grouping of trees on the mountains of Asia Minor. He designed a composition ideally suited to his own hilly Cotswold estate. Nearly one hundred years later, his far-sighted vision can be appreciated to the full; also his careful choice of lime-loving trees and shrubs for the heights, and clay-lovers for the lower lands of his estate.

At Batsford, there are superb arrangements whichever way you look. The dark green and sturdy European firs and the blue cedars contrast with the light green and more delicate growth of the silver birches and poplars. The arboretum spreads up the hill in front of the house to a height of 800 feet above sea level; here the incense cedars, natives of North America, have acclimatized to the cold Cotswold winds by adopting a columnar type of growth. A Buddha, in a posture of exhortation, presides up there, with a view of Moreton Vale and the distant Stow ridge. From a collection of nearly one thousand trees, I can only mention some of particular interest. I enjoy the variety of leaves to be seen at Batsford—the cut-leaved walnuts and beeches, the large leaves of Wilson's poplar, discovered by the explorer Wilson, a native of Chipping Campden—the feathery leaves of the nutmeg and the small leaves of the *Cereidiphyllum japonicum*. Of the rarer trees, there are the weeping form of the Serbian spruce, a native of the Carpathian Mountains, the tulip tree, with its delicate cup-like flowers, yellow autumn leaves and delicate aromatic scented bark. There are several Japanese walnuts and extraordinary contorted hazels. The Davidia, Chinese dove trees or handkerchief trees, are fascinating to see in May, when the pairs of white bracts, like fluttering wings or paper tissues, appear in order to protect the small flowers. Tree planting continues at Batsford under the direction of Lord Dulverton, the present owner. There is a scion of the famous mulberry from Shakespeare's garden in Stratford-upon-Avon, taken in 1923, many varieties of magnolias, japonicas and the South American Halesias or snowdrop trees, with their slender white flowers. The earliest-known tree is the ginkgo or maidenhair tree, a native of China. From fossilized remains it is established that it was a native of Europe millions of years ago. A fossilized leaf of a ginkgo was recently discovered at Naunton in the Cotswolds. The ginkgo was first reintroduced into Britain in the middle of the eighteenth century.

The gardens and arboretum at Batsford Park are open to the public during their spring and autumn perfection and to organized parties, on application to the head gardener.

After the glory of the trees, the church at the main gate of the park is disappointing, with its neo-Norman arches, the repetitive design of the wood carving, and the small private chapel, described by Goodhart Rendel as the "Holy Hon's Cupboard".

The garden at Sezincote, south of Moreton-in-Marsh, is unfortunately opened only once in the season, when the public may see the water garden designed by the topographical artist Thomas Daniell, also the park designed by Humphrey Repton, and marvel at the decorative architecture of the house. The original house was remodelled for the wealthy East India man, Sir Charles Cockerell, by his architect brother, Samuel Pepys Cockerell, who had the assistance of Thomas Daniell, a European knowledgeable on Indian architecture. The Prince Regent visited Sezincote in 1807 and his Brighton Pavilion was created seven years later. This pavilion, in its even more extravagant oriental style, seems less out of place in a seaside town that does Sezincote in its Cotswold surroundings. Thanks to the screens of well-grown trees in the large private park, this extraordinary building, with its onion-shaped dome and elaborate Indian exterior detail, now in no way obtrudes on the Cotswold landscape.

Beyond the house, a bridge with cast-iron Brahmin bulls on the balustrades carries the drive over the

A rest house in the arboretum at Batsford

landscaped valley, at the head of which is the Temple Pool, in front of an Indian shrine, which protects a stone relief of the goddess Souriya. Beside the clear waters of the pool is a collection of the scaly frilled shells of the giant clam, weathered to the same colour as the stone walls. The paths pass under the bridge, via a series of stepping stones, to the second pool with its tall fountain. Water issues from

225

the mouths of a three-headed serpent, its sinuous body coiled round a tree trunk. The stream flows on down the valley between beds of water-loving plants, the paths on either side criss-crossing the stream over giant-size, single-stone bridges. A group of ancient cedars graces the foot of the valley garden, where the stream is dammed up into a large pool before flowing down yet again to the long lake in the park.

Sezincote, a rare house to find hidden away in the Cotswolds

There is no need for a garden in front of the house. The ha-ha allows an uninterrupted view of the parklands sloping down to the lake and a distant view of Cotswold country. Well-wooded ground rises steeply behind the house, and the Indian styled orangery forms a long curved walk between the house and an elegant summerhouse. With so much water and many trees, it was not surprising to find the garden alive with birds—jays, collared doves, tree-creepers, fly-catchers and a heron by the lake, as still as the iron Brahmin bulls in the gardens. Far from still were the budgerigars in an aviary near the orangery—they were busy cheeping and fussing over the chicks they were raising. A pure white budgie, appeared quite distinguished amongst the bevy of yellows, greens and blues, proudly protecting her scruffy grey chick. A visit to Sezincote is a delightful and rare experience.

In the neighbouring village of Longborough, the church of St James passed to the Abbot of Hailes in 1325. In spite of the Victorian restoration, some Norman work survives. There are several monuments, one to a knight (dated 1325) and one to Sir Charles Cockerell (1837). The private Sezincote chapel was added to the church of St James after the demolition of Sezincote church and is approached by a private outside door, so cannot be seen with the rest of the church.

Beyond the church, on high ground, with a view across

Hidcote Manor, a late seventeenth-century house with a good buttressed stone barn and various elegant garden houses

the valley to Donnington, is a poorly conceived housing estate, appropriately named The Folly. Along the field path which leaves the small village green for Donnington, a large flock of gulls flew high above, like starlings making for a roosting place. Many of these small black-headed gulls have deserted the sea and become land birds, to enjoy the more lucrative pickings of the Cotswold country, but these normally noisy birds were silent; one rarely hears their seaside cries in the country.

The gardens surrounding the Cotswold Manor at Hidcote, which belongs to the National Trust, differ in layout from those at Sezincote. They are open five days a week throughout the season and are regarded as the botanical gardens of Gloucestershire. They were planned in 1903 by Major Laurence Johnston on the most unlikely site: bleak, cold, on the northerly Cotswold escarpment. It was to combat the cold winds that he conceived his idea of a series of small gardens protected by large hedges and, seventy years later, it is this variety of hedges which forms such a unique feature of the gardens. The small individual areas are symmetrically placed on an axis; the main vista walk, protected on the higher ground by a stilt hedge of hornbeam, slopes upwards from the house to a piered gateway. The individual gardens are so beautiful, with their pools, gazebos and rare plants, that one is apt to take for granted the far-sighted thought which prompted the

planting of the hedges. The mixed natural hedge, in yew, box, holly, beech and hornbeam, was a new idea when Major Johnston was planting, but is now well known amongst the gardening fraternity as a harlequin hedge.

As you pass through the top gateway, you leave behind the enclosed gardens and see a vast expanse of sky, the spread of the Avon valley and the distant Bredon Hill. The walk then descends under the ilex trees, past the tall ericas and shrub roses, down to the garden's own valley and small stream. The valley was planted with rare trees and shrubs and the banks of the stream with all kinds of water-loving plants.

On the right of the main vista walk is a large natural theatre with a semicircular grassy stage, backed by a high hedge and two beech trees, providing all the scenery necessary for a production of *As You Like It.* Further on, on the right are the large nursery and kitchen gardens, where the grass walks are edged with the old shrub roses, planted long before they returned to fashion. Varieties of clematis spill down from every dead fruit tree and the root stump of a Scotch pine has a halo of rock roses. Major Johnston, a keen botanist with aesthetic tastes, was no ordinary gardener. As V. Sackville West wrote: "He spilled his cornucopia everywhere", and that is the fascination of Hidcote. Flowers, shrubs and trees are allowed to spill over, to give of their best. The darkness of a sombre yew hedge is the ideal place for the scarlet flowers of the creeper *Tropaeolum speciosum* to spill over, as if they knew the yew provided the ideal background for their startling brilliance. A walk round Hidcote during any of the four seasons must be an inspiration to gardeners, professional or amateur. Whether you have acres or just a patch, there must be a wasted corner where a riot of colour could spill over and, as at Hidcote, the choice is yours, but the variety should be the best available. On a visit to Hidcote I came away with the philosophical advice from one of the gardeners: "Weeds! Don't 'ee let them get 'ee down. Weeds will grow, though it were in the middle of hell!" and in my nostrils was the "pungence of wood smoke, dearest of all earth's breathings" (Joan Murray Simpson.)

Along the lane, only a short walk from Hidcote Manor, are the gardens of Kiftsgate Court (open two days a week during the season). These are totally different in character and history from those at Hidcote. The beginning of the Cotswold escarpment starts to rise up behind Mickleton, towards the hamlets of Hidcote Boyce and Hidcote Bartrim. In 1750, when the poet and landscape gardener William Shenstone stayed at Mickleton Manor, there was a right of way from Mickleton to Hidcote Bartrim called Box Walk. Shenstone is believed to have inspired the planting of the many trees surrounding Box Walk, the Scots firs up the hillside and the two avenues of lime and elm. Shenstone's trees were well established before Kiftsgate Court was built in the late 1880s by Sidney Graves Hamilton of Mickleton Manor. People were able to indulge their fancies in those days, for labour was cheap. He had the entire Georgian façade of Mickleton Manor, which was to form the main feature of his new house on the hill, transported by a specially constructed light railway, which ran along the path under Shenstone's elms. It was as if he were afraid of not feeling at home up there, yet after the expenditure of so much effort, the Hamiltons only lived there until 1906.

The garden as we see it today was first conceived in the lifetime of Helen Muir, a keen botanist whose husband bought the estate in 1917. She was a life-long friend of her neighbour Major Johnston at Hidcote and accepted his good advice on planting. Apart from the interest of all the plants, shrubs and trees, the great attraction for me is the way in which the garden is planned to spread down the steep hillside towards Mickleton until the curved ha-ha finally separates it from the farmland below.

The idea of a ha-ha originated with Charles Bridgeman, who after years of training became royal gardener in 1728. When employed on the garden at Blenheim Palace, he conceived the idea of digging a ditch—a four-foot wall supporting the garden side and a gradual slope up into the adjoining field, as an effective device for excluding cattle

Kiftsgate Court

without interrupting the view. This idea was copied extensively by William Kent and Humphrey Repton when it became the fashion to dot the distant landscape with sham temples and ruins to serve as eye-catchers.

Struggling back up the extremely steep hillside garden at Kiftsgate, a few more terraces would ease the climb, I felt like the old lady who said her 'get-up-and-go' had 'got-up-and-went'.

When I have to leave the Cotswold country for work in a city, I leave it by way of these two great gardens which lie within the Kiftsgate Hundred and I bid farewell to the hills at the Kiftsgate Stone. The hundreds, a system developed by the Saxons for dividing large areas into districts, was so called because the areas originally each contained one hundred hides, or as much as would support one free family. The district surrounding Chipping Campden was originally in the Widless Hundred, which in the eleventh century became part of the much larger Kiftsgate Hundred, which covered much of Gloucestershire. The word 'gate' meant a steep valley or pass, and probably refers to the long ascent from Mickleton to Campden. This was the route of an ancient track which forded the Avon at Stratford and continued in a south-westerly direction, passing the traditional meeting place at the Kiftsgate Stone. At the stone, an open-air court was held once a month to see justice done, new customs

Kiftsgate Court. The fountain pool surrounded by the subtly planted white garden, with the rare white tree peony, Sufficosa Rock's variety, presented by the late Sir Frederick Stern

adopted and local affairs discussed. When the King's taxes were due, the King's representative was present. When direct speech was the only method of communication, all important proclamations were made at the stone. New taxes and new wars were announced, soldiers recruited and new kings proclaimed. The last new king to be

231

proclaimed at the Kiftsgate Stone was George III in 1760.

The old stone seems to have shrunk in size as well as in importance, due to centuries of sword-banging by overlords wishing to keep the attention of the athelings and serfs and impress upon them the importance of the latest announcement. More could be done to preserve and mark out this area, where the business of the county was conducted for centuries. The stone has weathered so many verbal and Cotswold storms; surely it has reached the ripe old age when it deserves a small pension to enable it to stand in dignified surroundings. For those wishing to pay their respects to the ancient stone, it stands just inside the wood at the top of Dyers Lane, nearly opposite the Cotswold Way as it takes to the high land above Chipping Campden, *en route* for Broadway. On every visit, I beat down the weeds and brambles surrounding the stone, and with laddered stockings reluctantly take my leave. For I never descend Dover's Hill with the same joyous enthusiasm I experience when I rush up to spend my time in Cotswold country.

The Kiftsgate Stone in Weston Park Wood. Conservationists, please save this ancient monument!

232

Index